INVISIBLE
MEN

INVISIBLE MEN

Mass Incarceration and the Myth of Black Progress

Becky Pettit

Russell Sage Foundation • **New York**

The Russell Sage Foundation

The Russell Sage Foundation, one of the oldest of America's general purpose foundations, was established in 1907 by Mrs. Margaret Olivia Sage for "the improvement of social and living conditions in the United States." The Foundation seeks to fulfill this mandate by fostering the development and dissemination of knowledge about the country's political, social, and economic problems. While the Foundation endeavors to assure the accuracy and objectivity of each book it publishes, the conclusions and interpretations in Russell Sage Foundation publications are those of the authors and not of the Foundation, its Trustees, or its staff. Publication by Russell Sage, therefore, does not imply Foundation endorsement.

Library of Congress Cataloging-in-Publication Data

Pettit, Becky, 1970–
  Invisible men : mass incarceration and the myth of black progress / Becky Pettit.
    p. cm.
  Includes bibliographical references and index.
  ISBN 978-0-87154-667-8 (pbk. : alk. paper) — ISBN 978-1-61044-778-2 (ebook)
1. African American prisoners.   2. African Americans—Social conditions.
    3. Discrimination in criminal justice administration—United States.   4. Criminal justice, Administration of—United States.   I. Title.
  HV9469.P46 2012
    365'.608996073—dc23   2012013794

Text design by Genna Patacsil.

RUSSELL SAGE FOUNDATION
112 East 64th Street, New York, New York 10065
10 9 8 7 6 5 4 3 2 1

entrepreneurial as my conscience as a social scientist allows. There will be some who believe I have gone too far and made questionable assumptions or indefensible assertions, and others who believe I have not gone far enough. I hope that this book will stimulate debate and that more comprehensive data collection will enable future scholars to investigate unresolved questions.

A great many people have had a hand in the production of this book. Bryan Sykes's energy and well-honed skills were vital to its completion. His work help lay the foundation for the book, and many of the empirical analyses reported in chapters 4, 5, and 6 are products of our collaborative efforts. Some of the key ideas have been developed in collaboration with my longtime collaborator and friend Bruce Western. Bruce has been an enduring supporter of this work and of the perspective I bring to it. There is no end to my respect for his intellectual integrity and my gratitude for his continued colleagueship. I am indebted to Jake Rosenfeld and Jennifer Laird, who were instrumental in the development of chapter 5, which draws heavily on our paper "Mass Incarceration and Voter Turnout" (Rosenfeld et al. 2010). And parts of chapter 4 are the result of collaborative work with Stephanie Ewert (Ewert, Sykes, and Pettit 2010). On this, and everything, it was a pleasure to work with Stephanie.

Patrick Denice provided excellent research assistance in the final writing stages. And I owe a great debt to Erin Powers. Despite all her other responsibilities, she took the time to edit this manuscript carefully. Her insights, as always, helped clarify the argument and make the manuscript more readable.

I am deeply grateful to friends and colleagues at the University of Washington, Northwestern University, the American Bar Foundation, and numerous other institutions who provided enthusiasm and critical feedback for this project. Specifically, I thank Katherine Beckett, Suzanne Bianchi, Traci Burch, Shawn Bushway, Bruce Carruthers, Sara Curran, Michael Dark, John Hagan, David Harding, Alexes Harris, Carol Heimer, Peter Hoff, Rucker Johnson, Meredith Kleykamp, Shelly Lundberg, Christopher Lyons, Ross Matsueda, Jane Mauldon, Ann Orloff, Devah Pager, Dylan Penningroth, Adrian Raftery, Steve Raphael, Lorna Rhodes, Jennifer Romich, Christopher Schmidt, Susan Shapiro, Herb Smith, Kate Stovel, David Takeuchi, Stewart Tolnay, and Chris Wildeman.

Bob Crutchfield's support and flexibility enabled me to focus my intellectual energy on this project when academic and administrative responsibilities demanded otherwise. Bob Nelson and the American Bar Foundation provided a wonderful working environment that facilitated the generation of the idea for this book and the completion of the final manuscript. James Cook deserves full credit for the subtitle. Suzanne Nichols of the Russell Sage Foundation shepherded me and this project as effectively as is imaginable. Her enthusiasm for this project was immensely productive, and I cannot thank her enough for her kindness and generosity.

There is no end to my gratitude for my wonderful family. In this, and all my other endeavors, they are unfailing in their support and encouragement.

There are countless others whom I have certainly forgotten. Their contributions are incalculable yet visible in the completed book, which would not have been written without them. All errors and omissions, however, remain my own.

CHAPTER 1

Invisible Men

I am invisible, understand, simply because people refuse to see me.
—Ralph Ellison, *Invisible Man* (1952)

On January 20, 2009, 1.8 million people of all races, colors, and creeds stood on the mall in Washington, D.C., to celebrate the inauguration of Barack Obama, America's first African American president. Journalists hailed the historic moment, and commentators from across the political spectrum questioned whether Obama's presidency marked the beginning of a postracial America. At the same time that the crowds in Washington watched Obama take the oath to uphold the Constitution, 2.3 million Americans sat invisible in America's prisons and jails, nearly half of them black.

The American prison system is both historically and comparatively unique. The United States now incarcerates a higher fraction of its population than at any other time in recorded history, and the United States leads the world in the percentage of its population held behind bars. Over one in one hundred American adults is living in a federal, state, or local prison or jail (Pew Research Center on the States 2008). If we include individuals on parole or probation, the numbers are even more startling. Nearly 5 million men and women are on probation, on parole, or under some form of community supervision. As a consequence, one in thirty-one American adults, or over 3 percent of the U.S. adult population, is under some form of correctional supervision (Glaze and Bonczar 2008). The Bureau of Justice Statistics estimates that if contemporary imprisonment rates continue, one out of every three black men will serve time in a federal or state prison (Bonczar 2003).

Criminals are under the near-constant gaze of the media. Gruesome crimes lead local television newscasts. Crime stories make newspaper headlines every day. Several large metropolitan-area newspapers devote whole sections of otherwise dwindling daily papers to crime reporting. Jonathan Simon (2007) has persuasively argued that since the declaration of war on crime in the 1960s, Americans have become increasingly fascinated with crime and criminality. Unabated press coverage of crime fuels fears of victimization and misperceptions about trends in crime. As a result, Americans have woefully inaccurate perceptions of their own risk of victimization and continue to believe that crime is on the upswing despite decades of declines in violent crime rates.

Just as criminals are under the gaze of the media and the public, individuals involved in the correctional system are closely supervised by correctional authorities. Some inmates face constant monitoring through video and other forms of surveillance in state-of-the-art supermax prisons (Rhodes 2004). Even inmates in minimum security facilities are continually supervised, repeatedly counted, and their movements carefully documented. Parolees and probationers are also routinely tracked through either electronic surveillance techniques or regularly scheduled meetings with parole and probation officers.

The intensive press coverage of America's criminals and the extensive supervision of inmates by correctional authorities belie the invisibility of inmates, parolees, probationers, and others involved in the criminal justice system to the outside world. Inmates are a social group isolated socially, physically, and statistically from much of the rest of society. The vast majority of our nation's inmates come from very few jurisdictions, and the facilities in which they are housed are even fewer in number (Heyer and Wagner 2004). Even our national data systems, as well as the social facts they produce, are structured around a normative kind of economic, political, and domestic life that commonly eludes those under the supervision of the criminal justice system.

Inmates and former inmates are less likely than otherwise similarly disadvantaged men to hold down steady legitimate jobs, to participate in civic life, and to live in settled households. Even their institutionalization involves a segment of the state cut off from the usual methods of social accounting. We categorically exclude inmates and former inmates from the social surveys routinely used to gauge the condition of the U.S. population, and we systematically undercount them in the U.S. Census and social surveys.

More than one hundred years ago, Émile Durkheim (1895/1982, 54) coined the term "social fact" to describe phenomena that both characterize and explain features of society: social facts are "the beliefs, tendencies and practices of the group taken collectively." In his own research, Durkheim commonly relied on statistics such as rates of births, marriages, or suicides to isolate and examine social facts.

This book documents how our collective blindness hinders the establishment of social facts, conceals inequality, and undermines the foundation of social science research, including that used in the design and evaluation of social policy. The decades-long expansion of the criminal justice system has led to the acute and rapid disappearance of young, low-skill African American men from portraits of the American economic, political, and social condition. While the expansion of the criminal justice system reinforces race and class inequalities in the United States, the full impact of the criminal justice system on American inequality is obscured by the continued use of data collection strategies and estimation methods that predate prison expansion.

BECOMING INVISIBLE

As Ralph Ellison so poignantly conveyed in his landmark book *Invisible Man* (1952), African Americans were socially invisible in pre–civil rights America. Racial discrimination, segregation, and exclusion contributed to a system of institutions, laws, and customs that maintained racial inequality and was premised on the subjugation and invisibility of African Americans (see, for example, Alexander 2010, 20–35). The civil rights era offered African Americans the promise of being accepted as visible citizens in American society. The Civil Rights Act (1964) and the Voting Rights Act (1965) signaled a new era of greater protections for the rights of African Americans and other groups, particularly in relation to education, employment, and voting.

The promise of the civil rights era has been undercut by a new form of invisibility manufactured by mass incarceration and the prison-industrial complex. Yet the invisibility of large segments of the American population and the inequality it conceals is not a natural or inevitable product of prison growth. In this book, I trace America's demographic charter to the constitutional mandate to conduct the decennial Census. I explore how the shifting demands of policymakers and researchers have led to increasing reliance on data collected from surveys of individuals living in households. I also document the impact of mass incarceration on the representativeness of individuals living in households. Incarceration is concentrated among the most disad-

how jail has made them invisible – put not a product of incarceration vantaged segments of the American population, and as a consequence those same individuals and social groups are invisible in many accounts of the U.S. population.

Chapter 2 begins by observing that since the founding of the United States the federal government has collected information every ten years in the decennial Census that documents the size and distribution of the population for the purposes of political apportionment. The U.S. Census Bureau and other federal data-collecting agencies have not always done a good job of collecting data on the full range of American experiences. Prior to emancipation, the number of slaves living in households was recorded on Census forms, yet no other information about them was collected, and they counted as only three-fifths of a person for the purposes of political apportionment. The repeal of slavery and the establishment of equal representation guaranteed by the Thirteenth and Fourteenth Amendments signaled the end of the "three-fifths compromise." Still, throughout much of the twentieth century African Americans were under-enumerated in U.S. population counts. Hispanics, Native Americans, and members of other minority groups have also been significantly under-enumerated at different points in American history (Anderson and Fienberg 1999; Snipp 1989, 2003).

Although there is evidence that the Census has improved its enumeration of blacks, Hispanics, and other minority groups, other methods of demographic and social data collection commonly used by the federal government are now increasingly problematic. Historical expansions of "grants-in-aid," most notably linked to the New Deal in the 1930s and the Great Society programs of the 1960s, accompanied an increased reliance by federal, state, and local governments on data about the condition of the population. Grants-in-aid commonly redistribute federal revenue to state and local governments. The amount of money allocated to local jurisdictions is often determined by formulas that include information about population size and characteristics provided by the Census and other federal data collection efforts. Since the 1930s, much of that data has been provided by surveys that are primarily restricted to people living in households, such as the Current Population Survey (CPS).

When the Current Population Survey was initiated in 1939 as the Sample Survey of Unemployment (Anderson 1988), incarceration rates were low and the exclusion of inmates from social surveys had relatively little consequence for the construction of social statistics. National surveys proliferated in the 1960s and 1970s along with the expansion of programs that employed grants-in-aid. Surveys initiated in the 1960s and 1970s adopted the same household-based sampling mechanism employed by the Current Population Survey, which categorically excludes the institutionalized and systematically undersamples the itinerant and homeless. To be sure, even at midcentury limiting sampling to individuals living in households excluded some subgroups of the population. Throughout most of the twentieth century and especially in the 1960s and 1970s, the largest group excluded was active-duty military.

Over the past thirty-five years, as the penal population has increased, surveys have not adapted their sampling frames to include the growing number of incarcerated Americans or itinerant former inmates. Today the size of the prison population far exceeds the size of America's active-duty military. The active-duty military population consists of approximately 1.4 million men and women who, in very broad terms, are generally representative of the American population (Government Accountability Office 2005; Kane 2005). The total inmate population now tops 2.3 million, and incarceration is so disproportionately concentrated among low-skill black men that it has become a routine life event for this demographic group (Pettit and Western 2004). As a consequence, penal system growth distorts accounts of the U.S. population derived from surveys that draw their samples from people living in households. Yet researchers, policymakers, and the public rarely consider the implications of our collective reliance on increasingly biased samples of the U.S. resident population generated by sample surveys of people living in households.

Chapter 3 engages with the idea that the public, policymakers, and researchers have not ignored inmates entirely. We are a culture fascinated by criminality, and newspapers and broadcast media are rife with images of crime and deviance. Once people are locked up in prisons or jails, however, they get less attention in the media until they are released, paroled, or furloughed. While there is little media coverage of former inmates who reintegrate into mainstream society after incarceration, repeat offenders are commonly featured in media accounts and political campaigns. Prominent policymakers—both Democrat and Republican—have made their careers out of being "tough on crime." And although Republicans claim much of the credit—or are targets of blame—for "tough on crime" legislation, Democrats have also been active proponents of the war on crime and the resulting penal expansion.

At the same time that the media has promulgated images of criminality and victimization, scholars have been slow to produce basic descriptive work documenting the scope of criminal justice expansion and the demographic contours of mass incarceration. We know, for example, that the prison and jail population has grown dramatically over the past thirty-five years. But we know less about the distribution of incarceration across social and demographic groups. For example, how has the composition of inmates changed over time? How do incarceration rates vary over time and in relation to gender, race, age, and indicators of social class like employment and education? How many people have ever spent time in a correctional facility or some other form of correctional supervision? How many people know, live with, or are related to someone who has been involved in the criminal justice system, and how is that experience distributed across the population?

Instead, scholarly attention has focused on calculating the behavioral implications of criminal justice contact. Administrative, survey, and experimental data have all been employed in an effort to estimate the outcomes of criminal justice contact and incarceration in the contemporary United States. For example, numerous studies have examined how criminal justice contact and incarceration affect employment and wage outcomes (Western 2002, 2006; Pager 2003, 2007; Apel and Sweeten 2010; Lyons and Pettit 2011). Other studies have investigated how the experience of incarceration affects voting and civic engagement (Uggen and Manza 2002; Manza and Uggen 2006; Burch 2010). And finally, a growing body of scholarship investigates how criminal justice contact influences family life, health, and community engagement (see, for example, Clear 2007; Foster and Hagan 2007; Geller, Garfinkel, and Western 2011; Geller et al., forthcoming; Massoglia 2008; Wildeman 2009).

Unfortunately, administrative and survey data are often narrow in scope, and the same data sets that fail to include current inmates in their samples commonly fail to collect data on prior criminal justice contact from the people they do interview. True experiments in the field are rare, and a measure of uncertainty clouds even the most rigorous studies. It is extraordinarily difficult, in a statistical sense, to identify the effects of incarceration on a range of life outcomes precisely because criminal justice contact and incarceration are disproportionately concentrated among certain subgroups of the American population. Research cannot easily sort out demographic from carceral effects. As a consequence, the findings of causally oriented research are continually debated, and fundamental questions about the effects of incarceration remain unresolved. Meanwhile, basic descriptions of the growth and distribution of criminal justice contact have received scant attention.

This book is designed to address some of the shortcomings of previous work through attention to the consequences for accounts of racial inequality in America of excluding inmates and former inmates from conventional data sources. Although the explicit goal of most censuses is to provide accurate population counts and the stated aim of most sample surveys is to be representative of a larger population, the rapid and dramatic growth in the U.S. criminal justice system has left key holes in accounts of the economic well-being, political engagement, and health status of the American population. The exclusion of the institutionalized from household-based surveys renders current inmates mute in statements of the American population's condition, and extremely high rates of residential instability and homelessness contribute to the invisibility of former inmates in official accounts of the population and its characteristics derived from the Census and household-based social surveys.

In Chapter 4, I illustrate how the exclusion of inmates from sample surveys profoundly influences the measurement of racial inequality in educational attainment, employment, and average wages. For example, there are significant discrepancies in estimates of the high school dropout rate between different data sources (see, for example, Heckman and LaFontaine 2010; Warren and Halpern-Manners 2009). Data from the Current Population Survey, meant to be representative of the U.S. population, places the high school dropout rate of young men at 13 to 16 percent and shows evidence of declines in the black-white gap in high school completion over the past few decades. Yet large urban school districts that are disproportionately black routinely report that 50 percent or more of their students drop out.

Although some discrepancy in measures from different data sources is to be expected because of the different aims of the surveys, the exclusion of inmates from the Current Population Survey, as Chapter 4 illustrates, contributes to a systematic bias in estimates of high school dropout rates. Inmates have extremely high dropout rates. Including inmates in estimates suggests a nationwide high school dropout rate among young black men more than 40 percent higher than conventional estimates using the CPS would suggest, and no improvement in the black-white gap in high school graduation rates since the early 1990s. Chapter 4 also reveals that similar bias affects conventional estimates of employment and wages. In 2008 nearly one in five young black men did not finish high school, black male dropouts were more likely to be in prison or jail than to be employed, and relative wages among young black men had seen little improvement over the previous twenty years.

In Chapter 5, I examine how decades of criminal justice expansion conceal racial inequality in voting. One of the most studied phenomena of contemporary American politics is the famous decline in voter turnout through the late 1990s. The decline in voter turnout was held to be particularly acute among whites, while voter turnout among African Americans held steady from the mid-1970s to the early 2000s. The twenty-first century has generally witnessed increases in voter turnout, especially among historically disenfranchised groups. The candidacy of Barack Obama has been linked to record high turnout among young African Americans. In chapter 5, I examine how trends in voter turnout are influenced by increases in incarceration. Although incarceration has undoubtedly disenfranchised large segments of the African American male population, incarceration also artificially inflates turnout rates among African American men because inmates and former inmates are underrepresented in surveys used to gauge trends in voting. Mass incarceration has narrowed the electorate sufficiently to generate an illusion of growing democratic engagement among young black men.

The effects of criminal justice expansion extend well beyond the lives of those incarcerated. Chapter 6 considers the impact of mass incarceration on children, families, and communities. Existing large-scale, national data collection strategies are not particularly well suited to address questions about the collateral consequences of decades of penal system growth. Surveys commonly used to gauge trends in American health and well-being, like the National Health Interview Survey (NHIS), the National Health and Nutrition Examination Survey (NHANES), and the National Survey of Family Growth (NSFG), adopted the same household-based sampling frame employed by the Current Population Survey. As a result, they also categorically exclude the institutionalized population and undersample former inmates with weak connections to households.

Although ethnographic and qualitative research has illuminated the broader effects of incarceration, we know less than we should about the aggregate impacts of incarceration on the health and well-being of inmates and their children, families, and communities owing to the limitations of existing survey data. In chapter 6, I piece together data from a number of different sources and review related research to illustrate the reach of incarceration into the lives of disadvantaged children and communities. This chapter shows that over 2.6 million children had a parent in prison or jail on any given day in 2008, as many as 12 percent of American children have had a biological father in prison or jail (Foster and Hagan 2007), and one-quarter of black children will experience parental imprisonment before their eighteenth birthday (Wildeman 2009). The extent of disadvantage that these children face is obscured because their parents—both fathers and mothers—are commonly underrepresented in social statistics. Likewise, existing data tell us relatively little about the impact of incarceration on the communities that inmates hail from and often return to, even though there is reason to believe that the consequences of mass incarceration for America's most disadvantaged communities are likely to be profound (see, for example, Rose and Clear 1998; Clear 2007).

The contemporary American criminal justice system is unique in both historical and cross-national perspective, and its implications for social science research and social policy are startling. Decades of penal system growth and high concentrations of incarceration among certain social and demographic groups skew comparative estimates of educational attainment (Heckman and LaFontaine 2010), employment (Western and Beckett 1999; Western and Pettit 2000), and wages (Western and Pettit 2005). Although there is reason to think that prison growth should influence myriad other social statistics, there is little evidence on that score.

This book provides a comprehensive examination of the effects of prison and jail growth on the construction of social statistics in a number of domains. In short, penal expansion has generated a class of citizens systematically excluded from accounts of the American populace. This exclusion raises doubt about the validity of even the most basic social facts and questions the utility of the data gathered for the design and evaluation of public policy and the data commonly used in social science research. As a consequence, we have lost sight of the full range of the American experience.

PENAL SYSTEM GROWTH IN THE UNITED STATES

When statistics on the size of the prison population were first recorded in 1925, 79 of every 100,000 Americans were held in federal or state prisons, generating an imprisonment rate of 0.079. The imprisonment rate, or the

Figure 1.1   U.S. Imprisonment Rate, 1925 to 2008

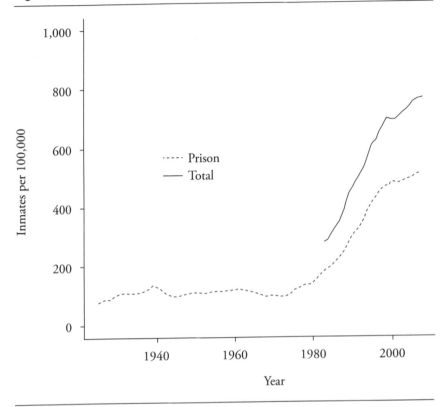

Source: Author's compilation based on data from U.S. Department of Justice (2009).
Note: Total includes inmates in prisons and jails.

percentage of Americans housed in federal or state prisons, hovered close to 0.1, or 100 in 100,000, until the mid-1970s. The long-term stability in the imprisonment rate prompted some prominent criminologists to claim the existence of a "natural" or stable incarceration rate (Blumstein and Cohen 1973).

Theories of stable incarceration rates were upended during the prison expansion that began in the mid-1970s (see figure 1.1). Between 1975 and 2009, the U.S. imprisonment rate grew at an average annual pace of 4.7 percent. This is a stunning increase considering that the imprisonment rate adjusts for population growth over the period. The incarceration rate, which includes inmates housed in local jails, grew almost as briskly, at 4.0 percent per year since 1982, when reliable data first became available.

By 2009, 2.3 million people were housed in America's prisons and jails (West and Sabol 2009; Minton and Sabol 2009). The U.S. imprisonment rate had reached 512 per 100,000, nearly six times the imprisonment rate that prevailed in 1925, when statistics were first reported. And if we include inmates housed in local jails, 768 of every 100,000 Americans were held in correctional facilities. Sociologist David Garland (2001) has coined the term "mass incarceration" to characterize the uniquely modern social phenomenon of extraordinarily high incarceration rates.

Mass incarceration is not only a contemporary development but also a distinctly American one. Until the mid-1970s, the incarceration rate in the United States was similar to the incarceration rate in France and Germany, among other industrialized nations (Whitman 2003). Even as recently as the mid-1990s, the United States lagged behind Russia in the proportion of the population held behind bars (Mauer 1994). Now, after more than three decades of penal expansion, the United States is the world leader in incarceration (International Centre for Prison Studies 2008). The United States outranks every other country for which there are available data on incarceration rates, including Rwanda, its closest competitor, which posted an incarceration rate approximately 80 percent of that of the United States (International Centre for Prison Studies 2008). Table 1.1 shows that in the mid-2000s the United States incarcerated a higher fraction of its population than any other advanced industrialized country. In fact, the incarceration rate in the United States is over ten times the incarceration rate in Sweden, Norway, Slovenia, Finland, and Denmark.

High incarceration rates are found throughout the United States. There is substantial variability in the proportion of the population that is incarcerated in different states, yet all U.S. states have incarceration rates that exceed those found in other advanced industrialized nations (figure 1.2). Thus, American prison growth is truly national in scope.

Decades after civil rights legislation provided for the social, economic, and political rights of people of color, race and class inequality in incarceration is at historic highs. To be sure, race and class disproportionality in incarceration rates reflects important differences in rates of offending (see, for example, Hawkins 2011). However, there is general agreement that the massive buildup in the size of the penal population has not been due to large-scale changes in crime or criminality. Instead, a host of changes at the local, state, and federal levels with respect to law enforcement and penal policy are implicated in the

Table 1.1   Incarceration Rates in Twenty-One Advanced
            Industrialized Nations, Mid-2000s

Country	Incarceration Rate (per 100,000 Total Population)
United States	760
Russian Federation	626
Poland	224
Czech Republic	201
Spain	162
Luxembourg	155
United Kingdom: England and Wales	152
Hungary	149
Australia	129
Canada	116
Netherlands	100
France	96
Austria	95
Belgium	93
Italy	92
Germany	88
Sweden	74
Norway	69
Slovenia	65
Finland	64
Denmark	63

Source: Author's compilation based on data from World Prison Brief database (International Centre for Prison Studies 2008).

expansion of the prison system. Law enforcement agencies have stepped up policing, prosecutors have more actively pursued convictions, and there have been myriad changes in sentencing policy that now mandate jail or prison time (Mauer 2006; Tonry 1995; Western 2006). However, while most scholars agree that "mass imprisonment" (Garland 2001) was not driven by increases in crime or criminality, there is no consensus explanation for the punitive turn in American criminal justice since the 1970s.

Figure 1.2   State Variability in Incarceration Rates per 100,000 Population, 2005

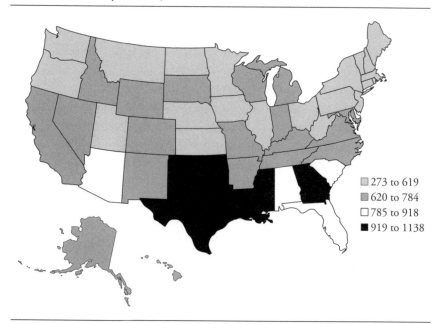

273 to 619
620 to 784
785 to 918
919 to 1138

Source: Author's compilation based on Beck and Harrison (2006), table 12.

Prevailing economic explanations for prison expansion have roots in Georg Rusche's conceptualization of the prison system as an institution to manage surplus labor (Rusche and Kircheimer 1939/2003). Arguments in this vein attribute the growth of incarceration to two sources. The first emphasizes the growth in the prison-industrial complex that is driven by demands stemming from the combination of prison guard unions, construction interests, and private security and prison firms that have a financial stake in the enterprise. The second argument cites a ready supply of poorly educated, mostly minority men turning to crime as a means of economic survival in a post-industrial economy. Empirical research has drawn connections between prison growth and the labor interests of corrections officers (Beckett 1997) and between high rates of incarceration among black and low-skill men and periods of labor inactivity (Western 2006).

Other scholars have persuasively argued that penal system growth must be considered in relation to a long history of racial inequality in the United States. For example, Loïc Wacquant (2000, 2001) draws attention to the racial aspects of social control by making historical parallels between the criminal justice system and other institutions that subordinated the interests of African Americans, such as slavery and Jim Crow. Michelle Alexander (2010) draws a number of parallels between the contemporary criminal justice system and Jim Crow segregation; she draws attention to how criminal justice policy and practice disproportionately affect African Americans in ways that undermine prospects for racial equality.

Political conditions have also been associated with prison policy, and the Republican Party plays a central role in explanations of prison expansion. Analysts commonly trace the beginning of the prison buildup to Barry Goldwater's elevation of crime and disorder as a campaign theme in the 1964 presidential election (Beckett 1997). Research also finds a positive correlation between the representation of Republicans in federal and state legislatures and the imprisonment rate (Jacobs and Carmichael 2002; Jacobs and Helms 1996). David Garland (1990) conceptualizes the penal system as a welfare institution—a government-sponsored effort to deal with society's failures.

Although Democrats may have been late to the "tough on crime" party, they were not immune to the punitive turn in American criminal justice policy. High incarceration rates are found throughout the country and even in strongly Democratic states with Democratic governors or Democrat-controlled legislatures. Highly visible Democratic Party leaders—from Bill Clinton to Joseph Biden—have endorsed "tough on crime" policies, and "tough on crime" legislation generally enjoys broad-based support. Such legislation, including policies that established a system of financial incentives associated with the seizure of property, both enable and encourage state and local jurisdictions to more strictly fight the war on drugs (Alexander 2010).

Although explanations for contemporary prison and jail growth remain a source of debate, growth of the criminal justice system itself is indisputable. Even in the face of steep crime declines through the 1990s, the penal system continued its historic expansion into the twenty-first century. Although women and Hispanics represent two of the fastest-growing segments of the incarcerated population, spending time in prison or jail continues to be most heavily concentrated among men, African Americans, and those with low skills, as indicated by their failure to complete high school (Western 2006). One in one hundred American adults is housed behind bars, yet the number for African American men is one in nine (Pew Research Center on the States 2008). The extent of race and class disproportionality in contemporary patterns of

Table 1.2   Civilian Incarceration Rates, Men Ages Twenty to Thirty-Four, by Education, 1980 to 2008

	1980	1990	2000	2008
White men				
Less than high school	2.4%	3.8%	7.7%	12.0%
High school	0.8	1.4	2.3	2.0
Some college	0.2	0.4	0.3	0.3
All	0.6	1.1	1.6	1.8
Black men				
Less than high school	10.6	19.6	30.2	37.2
High school	4.7	7.1	11.7	9.1
Some college	1.9	2.9	2.1	2.1
All	5.2	8.3	11.2	11.4

Source: Author's calculations. See the methodological appendix for details.

incarceration is striking. In the 1930s, blacks were three times more likely to be incarcerated than whites; in the 1990s the ratio increased to more than seven times that of whites (Duster 1997). As table 1.2 shows, incarceration rates among black men continue to be about seven times higher than those for whites. By 2008, the civilian incarceration rate among black men age eighteen to sixty-four was 8 percent, compared to 1.2 percent among non-Hispanic whites. Among young men between the ages of twenty and thirty-four, the incarceration rate for African American men was 11.4 percent, compared to 1.7 percent for non-Hispanic whites. Among those with the lowest levels of education, 37.2 percent of black men and 12 percent of white men were incarcerated.

The extreme disadvantage experienced prior to incarceration by prison and jail inmates can be seen in their extraordinarily low levels of educational attainment. Although there is some disagreement about the fraction of the U.S. population with a high school diploma (see, for example, Heckman and LaFontaine 2010; Warren and Halpern-Manners 2007, 2009; Warren 2005), estimates typically place the high school dropout rate close to 15 percent of the adult population. Table 1.3 indicates that by 2008 more than half of all male inmates—white, black, or Hispanic—between the ages of twenty and thirty-four had not completed high school. Among young, male, black in-

Table 1.3   Educational Distribution of Inmate Population, Men Ages Twenty to Thirty-Four, 1980 and 2008

	1980		2008	
	White	Black	White	Black
Less than high school	40.7%	52.7%	52.7%	61.8%
High school/GED	54.2	34.3	35.5	30.6
Some college	16.1	13.1	11.8	7.7

Source: Author's calculations. See the methodological appendix for details.

mates, more than six in ten had not completed high school or a general equivalency degree (GED). Between 1980 and 2008, as the overall educational attainment of the American population increased, the fraction of inmates with less than a high school diploma grew.

"Point in time" incarceration rates, which summarize the fraction of a given group that is incarcerated at any given time, are important determinants of the fraction of the population excluded from conventional household-based surveys. Surveys that draw their samples from people living in households categorically exclude inmates living in correctional institutions. The number and distribution of currently incarcerated individuals, then, is a key indicator of the characteristics of the population likely to be underrepresented in conventional accounts of the population that rely on surveys like the Current Population Survey.

At the same time, "point in time" incarceration rates only partially represent the total number of people at risk of undersampling in conventional surveys. Former inmates may be particularly likely to be excluded from social surveys that sample from households because they have high rates of residential mobility, instability, and homelessness (California Department of Corrections 1997; Morenoff, Harding, and Cooter 2009). Lifetime risks of imprisonment, therefore, may be an even better gauge of the size and distribution of the population rendered invisible in social statistics by the growth of incarceration.

The risk of imprisonment reflects the percentage of a specified population or group that can expect to serve time in prison before a given age. Table 1.4 indicates that the lifetime risks of imprisonment have also grown during the period of prison expansion. Moreover, the risks of imprisonment are increasingly concentrated among African American, low-skill men (see also Pettit

Table 1.4   Cumulative Risk of Imprisonment by Ages Thirty to Thirty-Four, 1979 to 2009

Year	All		Less Than High School		High School/GED		Some College	
	White	Black	White	Black	White	Black	White	Black
1979	1.4%	10.4%	3.8%	14.7%	1.5%	11.0%	0.4%	5.3%
1989	2.3	14.1	8.6	28.3	2.5	12.6	0.7	5.0
1999	3.8	21.5	14.4	46.0	5.0	20.2	1.0	6.6
2009	5.4	28.0	28.0	68.0	6.2	21.4	1.2	6.6

Source: Author's calculations. See the methodological appendix for details.

Notes: The 1979 cohort was born between 1945 and 1949; the 1989 cohort was born between 1955 and 1959; the 1999 cohort was born between 1965 and 1969; the 2009 cohort was born between 1975 and 1979.

and Western 2004). Five percent of white men and 28 percent of black men born between 1975 and 1979 spent at least a year in prison before reaching age thirty-five. The risks of spending time in prison for this birth cohort were significantly higher among high school dropouts: 28 percent of white and 68 percent of black dropouts had spent at least a year in prison by 2009.

Exposure to imprisonment now rivals or exceeds exposure to other social institutions long thought vital to the transition to adulthood, such as the completion of schooling, employment, or marriage. During the 2008 presidential campaign, Barack Obama was chided for saying that black men were more likely to go to prison than to go to college (see Alexander 2010, 185). Although his claim may seem to be far-fetched and to contradict notions of black progress, it was not too far from the truth. In fact, black men are more likely to go to prison than they are to complete college (Pettit and Western 2004). Spending time in prison has become more common than completing a four-year college degree or military service among young black men. And young, black, male high school dropouts are more likely to spend at least a year in prison than they are to get married. In short, among low-skill black men, spending time in prison has become a normative life event, furthering their segregation from mainstream society.

CONCLUSION

The criminal justice system and penal system growth fundamentally influence the construction of the social statistics commonly used in policy formulation and evaluation and in social science research. The disproportionate concentration of incarceration within particular social and demographic groups makes any portrait of the American social condition derived from these statistics incomplete, and it also obscures the extent of disadvantage within the groups where incarceration rates are highest. High rates of incarceration among black men—and black men with low levels of education in particular—have profound implications for accounts of their social standing and that of their children, families, and communities where they live prior to and following incarceration.

Data from the Census and ongoing federal surveys are routinely employed by policymakers and bureaucrats in Washington, D.C., in state governments, and in localities across the country. The Obama administration has repeatedly made the case for data-driven decision-making, congressional apportionment and redistricting hinge on the results from the 2010 Census, and lawmakers across the country use population estimates often provided by the federal government to design and evaluate a host of social programs. Yet 2.3 million or more Americans are overlooked as a matter of design in the most commonly used data sources, and they are undercounted in others.

Insofar as inmates differ in systematic ways from individuals living in households, data gathered through household-based surveys offer a biased glimpse into the American experience. The remainder of this book sheds light on the implications of this biased account for our understanding of black progress.

CHAPTER 2

Enumerating Inequality

We hold these truths to be self-evident, that all men are created equal, that they are endowed by their Creator with certain unalienable Rights, that among these are Life, Liberty, and the Pursuit of Happiness. That to secure these rights, Governments are instituted among Men, deriving their just powers from the consent of the governed.

—Thomas Jefferson, United States
Declaration of Independence (1776)

The routine collection of data about the American population was enshrined in the Constitution when the founders mandated the decennial Census. Social and economic data about the American population have been collected by the U.S. Census every ten years since 1790, but the Census has done an uneven job of accounting for everyone equally. One of the greatest contradictions in the history of American public policy is the incongruence between Jefferson's assertion of equal rights in the Declaration of Independence and the "three-fifths compromise" in the U.S. Constitution.

The Declaration of Independence offered the promise of equality and self-governance, but by ignoring the question of slavery and instituting the three-fifths compromise, the Constitution ensured inequality and denied the rights of certain groups of the population. Blacks were counted differently than other segments of the population until at least 1850, and they were not fully considered for the purposes of political apportionment until after the repeal of slavery in 1865. Today the data collected about the U.S. population have been expanded well beyond the population rosters and simple head-counts employed by the early Census-takers. The U.S. federal government and numerous other public and private organizations routinely employ a range of methods to gather data to assess the size and condition of the population for purposes of governance, commerce, and research.

Census-taking in the United States involves a complete population enumeration. Although the Census aims to count everyone in the population, the Census gathers relatively little by way of detailed information on the total population. Instead, social surveys, including the long form of the Census, the American Community Survey (ACS), and the Current Population Survey (CPS), employ statistical sampling to survey a relatively small subset of the population; gather detailed information on any measure of things, including the education, economic well-being, and health of that subset; and use the results to generalize about the condition of the larger population. Administrative records or registries are widely used in other countries, but in the United States are limited to individuals participating in specific programs, such as veterans, Social Security recipients, and licensed drivers. Administrative records, however, provide a wealth of data on social service use and other individual characteristics.

Information about population size, age distribution, geographic concentration, level of education, economic activity, and health is vital for the distribution of resources and the design of public and private services. Data collected through the Census, federal surveys that use statistical sampling, and administrative records help policymakers and private citizens decide when to build and where to site schools, hospitals, churches, roads, airports, universities, prisons, and a host of other public and private goods; in addition, demographic information on small geographic areas is commonly used to allocate federal funds. This same type of information is used by social scientists to describe features of society and theorize about human behavior and social processes.

Although the goal of most censuses is to provide accurate population counts and the aim of most sample surveys is to be representative of a larger population, the rapid and dramatic growth in the U.S. penal system has led to incomplete and inaccurate accounts of the condition of the American population measured by sample surveys. The effects of the criminal justice system on our perception of American inequality have now reached historic proportions. The first U.S. Census documented 3.9 million people (Anderson and

Fienberg 1999). Today over half that number reside in federal, state, or local prisons and jails, and almost twice that number are under the surveillance of the criminal justice system (West and Sabol 2009; Glaze and Bonczar 2008).

At the nation's founding, the three-fifths compromise required that slaves be considered three-fifths of a free person for the purposes of apportionment (Anderson and Fienberg 1999), making as many as 40 percent of African Americans invisible. Although slaves and free blacks were enumerated on household rosters, little information about them was collected—not even their age and gender—until the Census of 1850. The scant information collected about many American blacks obscured their experience for much of American history; evidence suggests that they were hardly considered in the design or evaluation of public policy. Similarly, the dramatic growth of imprisonment in the United States since the 1970s has resulted in historically unprecedented numbers of Americans whose experience goes uncounted, much less considered. This chapter details how inmates became invisible and documents their number and distribution.

THE HISTORY OF ENUMERATION

Article 1, section 2, clause 3, of the U.S. Constitution stipulates:

> [Representatives and direct Taxes shall be apportioned among the several States which may be included within this Union, according to their respective Numbers, which shall be determined by adding to the whole Number of free Persons, including those bound to Service for a Term of Years, and excluding Indians not taxed, three fifths of all other Persons.] The actual Enumeration shall be made within three Years after the first Meeting of the Congress of the United States, and within every subsequent Term of ten Years, in such Manner as they shall by Law direct.

The first U.S. Census was conducted in 1790 under the auspices of the executive branch through the Department of State (Anderson 1988). In many ways, census-taking in 1790 was very similar to contemporary census-taking. In 1790 the census-taker collected information for each household about the number of free white males over and under age sixteen, free white females, other free persons, and slaves (Anderson 1988). Today, in addition to information on individual household members provided by household heads, the Census also relies on administrators of group quarters, including prisons and jails, mental health facilities, and long-term care facilities, to report on the residents of their facilities. Some effort is made to account for those not otherwise counted, such as unresponsive households, the homeless, and transients (Anderson and Fienberg 1999; Citro, Cork, and Norwood 2004).

Prior to the abolishment of slavery in the Thirteenth Amendment and the establishment of due process and equal protection provided by the Fourteenth Amendment, the large fraction of the U.S. population who were slaves were counted differently than the rest of the population. Although not all black Americans were slaves, evidence suggests that Census enumerators often miscategorized free blacks as slaves (Anderson 1988). Very little information was collected about slaves beyond how many there were within a household.

The lack of information about blacks generally and about slaves in particular in early American censuses generated a fundamental form of exclusion. The three-fifths compromise led to the exclusion of as many as 40 percent of black Americans from consideration in the apportionment of congressional seats, at least through the Census of 1860. In addition, the African American experience was relegated to second-class status in the social register, the historical record, and, presumably, the public mind. Historians have painstakingly reconstructed some aspects of African American economic and social life using a wide variety of historical data, including diaries, writings, church registries, and legal records. Yet the Census tells us remarkably little about the social life of American blacks until at least 1850, when the names of all free blacks were recorded in the Census and the Census began to collect more information about slaves (U.S. Census Bureau 2008a). It was not until 1870 that the Census included the names of all African Americans on Census forms (U.S. Census Bureau 2008a).

Section 2 of the Fourteenth Amendment to the U.S. Constitution provides for the full consideration of African Americans for the purposes of apportionment. However, states were allowed to apportion legislative districts with wildly disproportionate populations until the U.S. Supreme Court, in Baker v. Carr (369 U.S. 186 1962), interpreted the amendment to require one-person, one-vote apportionment. In theory, by 1870 Census-takers were supposed to count blacks in the same manner as whites and to collect comparable social and demographic information regardless of race. However, nearly 150 years after Reconstruction, there is widespread evidence that African

Americans are consistently undercounted by the Census (Preston et al. 2003) and growing evidence that the full range of their experience is concealed by other methods of data collection, including the now-popular sample survey.

In the nineteenth century, scholars from a range of disciplines recognized that the kind of data the Census provided did not adequately represent the living and laboring conditions in rapidly changing societies. Moreover, policymakers found that Census data often did not provide the information necessary for growing policy demands. Critics may question the effectiveness of social survey research for policy formulation, but statisticians, public health officials, and social reformers, responding to industrialization, urbanization, and westward expansion, needed to survey the population and its condition. Typically they did so through small area studies, which often drew attention to the experiences of the poor (Converse 1987).

At the same time, significant advances were made in the field of statistics in the use of social survey research to study human populations. The Statistical Society of London, later to become the Royal Statistical Society, was founded in 1834 and included the likes of Thomas Malthus and Adolphe Quetelet (Bulmer, Bales, and Kish-Sklar 1991). Malthus's alarmist views on the impacts of population growth not only were provocative but drew attention to the need to regularly gather information on the population for resource planning and distribution. And although Quetelet's theories about the social condition were strikingly deterministic, his pioneering work on probability would have great influence on the development of probabilistic sampling and theories of statistical inference (Bulmer, Bales, and Kish-Sklar 1991).

The utility of observation and household surveys for research was exemplified by John Snow's work on cholera in London in the mid-1800s. Snow's investigation into the 1853–1854 cholera epidemic involved observations and surveys to ascertain from which water company households obtained their drinking water (Freedman 1991). Snow's careful empirical work not only demonstrated that cholera was a waterborne illness, but also laid the foundation for studies of local areas. Later in the nineteenth century, students of the British and American social condition conducted local social surveys that provided revealing details of social life in cities, such as Charles Booth's surveys in London and W. E. B. DuBois's in Philadelphia (Bulmer, Bales, and Kish-Sklar 1991; Converse 1987).

By the late nineteenth century, decennial Census data and other data collected by the federal government had many uses beyond congressional apportionment and taxation; some of those uses were prescribed by law, while others were artifacts of common practice. In the late 1800s, the federal government began the practice of distributing money to states and eventually localities through a practice known as "grants-in-aid." The first national grants-in-aid were land grants set aside for public universities. Later grants-in-aid would be used to allocate additional resources for education, unemployment insurance, housing assistance, road construction, and a host of other public goods (Dommel 1974).

Detailed information about the composition and economic capacities of the U.S. population became increasingly relevant with the growth of grants-in-aid. The federal government, states, and localities were keen to document the composition of various constituencies in order to allocate grants-in-aid. The Census of 1890 expanded significantly to address some of these new data needs. By 1902, when the Census Office became permanent—initially as part of the Department of Interior, but then it was transferred within a year to the newly created Department of Commerce and Labor—detailed social and demographic information about the population was a mainstay of public discourse and policy debate, particularly in relation to the fortunes of the poor and the status of American workers (Anderson 1988).

Shortly after the Commerce Department assumed responsibility for conducting the decennial Census, there was yet another significant change in its mission. Passage of the Sixteenth Amendment in 1913 allowed Congress to levy an income tax without regard to apportionment among states or Census results. As a consequence, ever since 1913 the primary and only constitutionally mandated purpose of the Census has been congressional apportionment. Nonetheless, social and demographic data were in high demand—and continue to be—for both policymaking and research needs.

It was not until more than a half-century after the first grants-in-aid were distributed that sample surveys were routinely used in government policy formulation. The New Deal legislation of the 1930s allocated federal funds to state and local governments that were targeted for specific aims, including infrastructure development and public assistance (Anderson 1988). Detailed data about the population became essential not simply to resolve the controversy between the Hoover and Roosevelt administrations about the depth of the Depression, but also to help target resources effectively.

Those called upon to provide information about the economic condition of the population quickly realized that they had to expand the common methods of data collection in order to have enough information available, at regular intervals, to be useful. Federal revenue-sharing through grants-in-aid required even more information, and at shorter intervals than what was already available through the decennial Census. The expansion of grants-in-aid during the Depression demanded exactly the kinds of data that statistically based sampling might afford. Rather than waiting every ten years for the results of the Census, statistically based sampling offered the possibility of collecting detailed data on small though representative segments of the population at shorter intervals.

Despite great interest in inter-Census estimates of unemployment and other measures, there was some controversy over how to gather the information. Statisticians had made important advances in statistical sampling theory and methods, yet policymakers were reluctant to sponsor sample surveys. During the height of the Depression, the newly constituted Central Statistical Board sponsored a small three-city study of unemployment to test the feasibility of using a sample survey to gauge the economic condition of the American population. Although that survey and others, including a postal enumeration of the unemployed, helped advance the statistical methodology involved in implementing national sample surveys, political resistance lingered (Anderson 1988).

Nonetheless, in 1939 the Works Progress Administration (WPA) conducted the first Sample Survey of Unemployment, a monthly, national sample survey (Anderson 1988). The survey drew its sample from individuals living in households and categorically excluded people living in institutions like prisons, jails, hospitals, and military barracks. The household-based survey provided rich and detailed information on the economic and social condition of the American population. The survey survived the abolishment of the Works Progress Administration, was transferred to the Census Bureau in 1942, and in 1947 was renamed the Current Population Survey (Anderson 1988). The CPS continues to be a primary data collection tool to report on the condition of the population and to construct the small-area inter-Census estimates used in policymaking.

The concept of proportional representation—and proportionality more generally—guided much policymaking through the latter half of the twentieth century. The "equal protections" clause in title 2, section 2a, of the U.S. Code created individually based rights and was associated with a symbolic shift toward proportionality. It therefore became even more important when

Table 2.1   Federal Grants-in-Aid to State and Local Governments, 1940 to 2008

Year	Current Dollars (Millions)	Constant Dollars (Billions)	Percentage of Federal Outlays	Percentage of GDP
1940	$872	$11.4	9.2%	0.9%
1950	2,253	17.2	5.3	0.8
1960	7,019	39.0	7.6	1.4
1970	24,065	105.3	12.3	2.4
1980	91,385	192.6	15.5	3.3
1990	135,325	172.1	10.8	2.4
2000	285,874	285.9	16.0	2.9
2008 (estimated)	466,568	367.4	15.9	3.3

Source: Author's calculations based on U.S. Census Bureau (2008b), table 0414.

allocating representation, goods, or services to have an accurate count of the size and composition of the population, its characteristics, and its capacities.

It is perhaps not coincidental that the two periods in American history that witnessed the greatest growth in the transfer of federal money to the states through grants-in-aid were also boom years for federal data collection about the population. Under Roosevelt's watch during the Great Depression and during the Great Society programs of the Johnson administration, the amount of federal aid to state and local governments through grants-in-aid expanded dramatically. The amount of federal money allocated to the states more than quadrupled in the first two years of the Roosevelt administration. The 1960s witnessed the greatest expansion of government revenue-sharing in absolute and percentage terms since the 1920s. Revenue-sharing went from just shy of $8 billion in 1962 to almost $36 billion by 1972 (Dommel 1974). Table 2.1 tracks grants-in-aid since 1940.

Until the Great Society programs of the Johnson administration in the 1960s, grants-in-aid had fallen into two major functional categories: transportation and public assistance (Brown, Fossett, and Palmer 1984). However, the Johnson administration—and the later administrations of Nixon, Ford, Carter, and Reagan—expanded grants to the states in a wide variety of areas, including health, education, employment and labor, housing, and even crime control. This new function-oriented approach to governance required additional data collection for both program design and program evaluation (Anderson 1988). There was an attendant proliferation of surveys administered by different governmental agencies employing statistical sampling methods.

Table 2.2 is a partial list of major surveys administered by the federal government and initiated since the Sample Survey of Unemployment became the Current Population Survey in 1947. Many of these surveys are ongoing and continue to frame our social scientific understanding of the American population and guide the allocation and evaluation of public services. Most of them draw their samples from individuals living in households. The National Longitudinal Surveys and related surveys that have followed—including the National Longitudinal Survey of Youth 1979 and 1997 (NLSY-79 and NLSY-97)—draw their samples from birth cohorts. In the NLSY-79 and NLSY-97, attempts are made to interview respondents while they are in prison or jail. The National Adult Literacy Study (NALS) is one of the very few studies that seeks to interview a sample of prison inmates. And although the American Community Survey (ACS) was initially restricted to people living in non-institutionalized households, it now includes interviews with people living in group quarters.

Despite all the changes affecting the use of the decennial Census and the proliferation of other data-gathering methods, the central role of the decennial Census in enumerating the population for purposes of political apportionment was upheld in Supreme Court rulings as recently as 1999 (U.S. Department of Commerce vs. U.S. House 525 U.S. 316, 334–36, 1999). Although court decisions have barred the use of sampling for apportionment, methods that include statistical sampling and statistical adjustment can be used for congressional redistricting and the allocation of federal funds through general revenue-sharing and grants-in-aid. Contemporary estimates shown in table 2.1 suggest that 16.1 percent of the federal budget and 3.3 percent of U.S. gross domestic product are allocated to state and local governments through such programs; much of the allocated money is linked to data collected through the Census and through sample surveys about population size and characteristics (Anderson 1988).

ESTIMATING HARD-TO-REACH POPULATIONS

The overall size and percentage of the decennial Census undercount have diminished since midcentury; the undercount is still notably large among particular social and demographic groups, however, and some groups have with-

Table 2.2   Major Sample Surveys Administered by the Federal Government, 1947 to 2003

Survey	Year Initiated	Sampling Frame	Department
Current Population Survey (CPS)	1947	Household (HH) non-institutionalized	Commerce
National Health Interview Survey (NHIS)	1957	HH	Health and Human Services (DHHS)
National Health and Nutrition Examination Survey (NHANES)	1959	HH	DHHS
National Longitudinal Surveys (NLS)	1966	Birth cohorts	Labor
National Survey of Drug Use and Health (NSDUH)	1971	HH	DHHS
National Survey of Family Growth (NSFG)	1973	HH	DHHS
National Crime Victimization Survey (NCVS)	1973	HH	Justice (Bureau of Justice Statistics)
Medical Expenditure Panel Survey (MEPS): Household Component	1977	HH	DHHS
Survey of Income and Program Participation (SIPP)	1983	HH	DHHS/Agriculture, conducted by Census Bureau
National Longitudinal Studies of Aging (NLSA)	1984	HH	DHHS (National Institute on Aging)
National Adult Literacy Study (NALS)	1992	HH and prison	Education
Survey of Program Dynamics (SPD)	1997	HH	DHHS/Agriculture, conducted by Census Bureau
American Community Survey (ACS)	2003	Population	Commerce

Source: Author's compilation.

Table 2.3   Estimated Net Census Undercount from 1940 to 2000

Year	Black	Non-Black	Difference	Overall Net Undercount
1940	10.3%	5.1%	5.2%	5.6%
1950	9.6	3.8	5.8	4.4
1960	8.3	2.7	5.6	3.3
1970	8.0	2.2	5.8	2.9
1980	5.9	0.7	5.2	1.4
1990	7.4	1.0	6.4	1.9
2000	2.8	−1.2	4.0	0.1

Source: Author's calculations based on data from Anderson and Fienberg (1999) and Robinson, West, and Adlakha (2002).

stood inclusion. For example, research comparing military enlistment records and Census data suggests that, in 1940, 2.8 percent of draft-eligible men were not included in the Census but enlisted for military service (Price 1947). Among African Americans, the undercount was over 300 percent higher: 13 percent of draft-eligible black men went uncounted by the decennial Census (Price 1947). Recent assessments of the conduct of the 2000 Census find that the overall undercount was quite small by historical standards, but that as many as 3 percent of African Americans were nevertheless not included in population counts (Robinson, West, and Adlakha 2002; see also table 2.3). Perhaps even more remarkable, however, is that 5 percent of black men are estimated to have been excluded from the 2000 Census counts (Robinson et al. 2002).

Exactly why African Americans in general—and black men in particular—continue to elude census-takers in such great numbers is a deep question that occupies a great deal of scholarly and policy research. Some explanations for the persistence of the undercount among African Americans suggest that long-standing and deep-seated mistrust of government among some minority groups is associated with higher rates of refusal to participate in census-taking endeavors (Anderson and Fienberg 1999). More prevalent, however, are explanations that suggest that African Americans and other minorities are disproportionately, though unintentionally, missed in the Census because of the circumstances in which they live (Anderson and Fienberg 1999). Higher rates of residential mobility and instability, homelessness, and residence in highly concentrated urban areas are associated with a greater risk of under-enumeration

(Anderson and Fienberg 1999); those same experiences are highly correlated with spending time in prison and jail (Morenoff, Harding, and Cooter 2009; California Department of Corrections 1997). Recent research by Alice Goffman (2009) persuasively demonstrates how young black men in Philadelphia elude identification by formal authorities and eschew formal attachments to work and family in an effort to avoid spending time in jail. This suggests that the criminal justice system itself may exacerbate the under-enumeration of the most disadvantaged segments of the population.

Strangely enough, evidence suggests that recently the Census does a poor job enumerating men known to be in prison or jail at the time of the survey (Citro et al. 2004). Between 1980 and 2000, Census estimates of the institutionalized population closely approximated the numbers of inmates in prison or jail provided by the Bureau of Justice Statistics. Census data not only matched up with BJS numbers in the aggregate but also provided comparable estimates of inmates within race and education groups. In recent years, however, there has been a dramatic divergence in estimates of the prison and jail population provided by the Census Bureau through the American Community Survey and the Bureau of Justice Statistics. For example, in 2006 ACS data indicated that 7.5 percent of white male dropouts and 29.0 percent of black male dropouts were in some type of institution, while estimates constructed using BJS data place 10.7 and 36.0 percent of the same groups, respectively, in prison and jail.

Although there is widespread agreement that prison and jail represent the overwhelming majority of institutionalization of young men, it is unclear why the Census should generate estimates of the institutionalized population that differ so greatly from the Bureau of Justice Statistics estimates. Divergence between estimates is even greater in 2007, which is the last year for which comparable data are available. In addition, data collected in 2006 and 2007 through the American Community Survey show a decline since 2000 in the number and percentage of white and black men ages twenty to thirty-four incarcerated in American correctional facilities, although other sources, including the Bureau of Justice Statistics, point to continued albeit slowed growth in incarceration over the period. There is concern that Census data collection efforts have not kept pace with prison expansion, causing an undercount among prison inmates (Citro et al. 2004).

Other social surveys that employ statistical sampling do no better at including black men in assessments of the population. In fact, they do much worse, primarily because nearly all federal sample surveys of the population draw their samples from individuals living in U.S. households (Siegel and Swanson 2004). As the prison system has grown, and to the extent that it is disproportionately composed of men, African Americans, and those with low levels of education, surveys that exclude the institutionalized do not accurately represent the experiences of the general population. Household-based surveys that categorically exclude the incarcerated population ignore fully one in nine black men between the ages of twenty and thirty-four. Among black men with less than a high school diploma, whose incarceration rates are highest, over one-third of the population is excluded by design from sample surveys of non-institutionalized persons living in households.

A secondary reason why survey research fails to represent the full range of the American experience is that a large number of young black men are likely to be overlooked by household-based sample surveys because they maintain tangential connections to households (see, for example, Goffman 2009). Combining the number of currently incarcerated men with the number of non-institutionalized men who go uncounted by the Census because of nonresponse or nonlocation suggests that 16 percent or more of black men are invisible in conventional accounts of the population.

Despite general improvements in Census coverage over the past half-century, African Americans continue to be undercounted by wide margins, and black men in particular are the most likely to be missed. High rates of incarceration among black men may further hinder future prospects for their enumeration. At the same time, sample survey research, including the Census's own American Community Survey, has not kept pace with the changes in American demographics wrought by the prison buildup. The concentration of incarceration and exclusion from household-based survey research among black men with low levels of education is startling. The omission from the Census and sample surveys of large segments of the population concentrated within particular social and demographic groups clearly has consequences for political apportionment and the allocation of public resources. Their exclusion also obscures the establishment of the fundamental social facts—including the needs and capacities of the population—that frame our understanding of the American condition.

CONCLUSION

The invisibility of American inmates is a product of America's demographic charter enshrined by the Constitution, designed by various federal agencies, and upheld by the U.S. Supreme Court. Over the past two hundred years, the federal government has kept pace with advances in survey methodology and expanded and updated its data collection efforts in order to enhance the design of public policy and guide the allocation of goods and services. While its history is rich, the decennial Census is now primarily used for congressional reapportionment. And from humble beginnings as the Sample Survey of Unemployment, the Current Population Survey is now widely used by a range of federal agencies. Researchers have spent countless hours using the CPS to construct trends over time in unemployment, voter turnout, health, and myriad other measures to better understand the economic, political, and social condition of the American population.

Unfortunately, the Current Population Survey and most other federally administered sample surveys have failed to keep pace with a rapidly expanding criminal justice system. The dramatic expansion of the criminal justice system since the early 1970s and its disproportionate encapsulation of low-skill minority men have had profound effects on inequality in a host of domains. Yet we are only beginning to understand the magnitude of those effects because those same men and their circumstances are undercounted in Census data and excluded from survey research using household-based samples.

The remaining chapters of this book illustrate the implications of the exclusion of inmates from social survey research and accounts of social inequality. In summary, research that relies on data from the Census and household-based sample surveys misrepresents the American social condition, especially as it concerns African American men. Conventional survey data overstate levels of education, economic well-being, political participation, and social integration of African American men. The exclusion of the prison and jail population creates an illusion of black progress and obscures the continuation of racial inequality well into the twenty-first century.

CHAPTER 3

Under Surveillance

Everything that we see is a shadow cast by that which we do not see.
—Martin Luther King Jr., *The Measure of a Man* (1958)

In 1981, in the early years of America's experiment in mass incarceration, a feature story called "The Curse of Violent Crime" ran in *Time* magazine. The article cited a number of alarming statistics: "Every 24 minutes, a murder is committed somewhere in the U.S. Every ten seconds a house is burgled, every seven minutes a woman is raped. . . . roughly one out of every three households in the U.S. was directly affected by some kind of serious crime last year." The article vividly portrayed the experiences of victims and their survivors by drawing attention to crimes involving children abducted and killed by strangers, repeated burglaries, rape, murder, and carjacking: a veritable "surge of mindless cruelty." In the article, Harry Scarr, a former director of the Bureau of Justice Statistics, predicted: "Within four or five years every household in the country will be hit by crime" (Magnusson 1981).

In the decades since Scarr's bold prediction, the country has experienced both increases and decreases in violent crime. Yet media coverage of crime does not generally track the incidence of crime. Disproportionate media attention to violent crime has important implications for perceptions of the risk of victimization and public support for continued expansion of the American criminal justice system. In fact, although crime is now near historic lows, accounts of crime and victimization continue to fill the national and local print and broadcast media.

The adage "if it bleeds, it leads" characterizes media coverage of the criminal justice system in a society both fascinated and repulsed by criminality and in which widely disproportionate attention is paid to relatively rare crimes like stranger abductions, serial killings, multiple murders, and crimes where the perpetrator is unknown to the victim. Research suggests that crime stories account for 75 percent or more of all local television news in some cities and that, more often than not, local television stations begin their newscasts with a story about crime (Klite, Bardwell, and Saltzman 1997). One only needs to turn on the local TV news for a graphic depiction of violence and brutality in contemporary America.

Even the frequency of crime-related stories in local papers can be quite alarming. In many small and medium-sized towns across America, crime stories top the local news day after day. Newspapers in major metropolitan areas devote whole sections to coverage of crime-related issues. The *Los Angeles Times* includes a "Homicide Report" that identifies all known homicide victims in the Los Angeles area and includes details on the location and circumstances surrounding their death. The *Milwaukee Journal-Sentinel* includes a "Most Wanted" section that identifies alleged criminals being sought by the police. And reminiscent of the TV drama *Cold Case,* the online version of the *Dallas Morning News* includes links to video profiles of unsolved cases being investigated by the Dallas Police Department's cold-case squad.

The broadcast and print media are not just filled with gruesome stories about the latest death or abduction; they also translate the official crime statistics periodically released by federal, state, and local authorities and report on the politics and business of crime and criminal justice. Every year numerous stories recount the growth (or decline) in crimes reported to the police and the number of people reporting criminal victimization. In election years, the news is filled with reporting on the stances on crime and crime control of political aspirants. Major legislative changes in criminal justice policy and judicial rulings about crime-related issues like gun control also attract significant media attention.

The visibility of crime in the United States and the near-constant surveillance of inmates (to be detailed later in this chapter) contrast sharply with the social marginality of men who are and have been incarcerated. Inmates and former inmates are largely below the radar of mainstream social institutions. Prison growth has produced a class whose living arrangements both inside and outside of prison reflect deep powerlessness and whose members are of-

Figure 3.1   Number of Stories Including the Phrase "Violent Crime" in the *New York Times*, 1970 to 2009

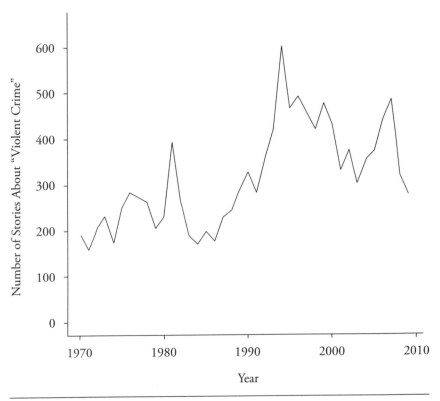

Source: Author's compilation based on search of *New York Times* archive (2010).

ten not even counted, much less considered, in the formulation of social policy or social science research unless it directly pertains to criminal justice.

THE VISIBILITY OF CRIME AND CRIMINALS

One might imagine that the number of news stories about issues related to crime or criminal justice might rise and fall along with crime rates. On the contrary, the amount of attention to these issues in the American media bears only a modest resemblance to trends in crime. Figure 3.1 shows the number of stories appearing in the *New York Times* each year from 1973 to 2009 that included the phrase "violent crime." Violent victimization rates grew from the early 1970s through 1981, with the murder rate peaking in 1980. The number of stories about violent crime ranged from two hundred to three hundred between 1973 and 1980. Attention to violent crime in the pages of the *New York Times* surged in 1981 when, as the *Time* article suggests, Americans were captivated by violent crime.

Not coincidentally, in 1981 Attorney General William French Smith instituted the Task Force on Violent Crime, which received quite a lot of media attention. Smith's task force ultimately offered sixty-four recommendations in response to its charge to investigate what additional steps the federal government could take to combat violent crime (Reid 1982). Many of those recommendations were designed to increase the capacity of the criminal justice system and promote incarceration: to build new prisons, to institute determinant sentencing, and to enable long periods of pretrial detention, among other things. Although the report itself was subject to intense scholarly criticism, many of its recommendations were swiftly adopted across the country (see, for example, Thompson 1982).

After the squall surrounding the efforts of Smith's task force subsided, media coverage of violent crime retreated to pre-1981 levels for much of the 1980s. But by the end of the decade, there was growing attention to violent crime in the news and a steady uptick in the number of stories related to crime and victimization. The 1994 Crime Bill (HR 3355 Public Law 103-322) attracted the attention of both the left and the right and fueled a significant number of media reports. The bill was originally written by Sen. Joseph Biden of Delaware and sponsored by Democratic representative Jack Brooks of Texas before he lost his reelection bid in 1994. It received widespread, though not unanimous, support from both Democratic and Republican legislators at a time when it was politically advisable to be viewed as tough on crime. The Crime Bill's provisions included federal support for additional police officers at the local level, the establishment of new federal crimes, truth in sentencing statutes, a federal ban on assault weapons, and the elimination of Pell grants for convicted felons, among other things. In 1994, during the height of debate about the Crime Bill, six hundred stories about violent crime—nearly two per day—appeared in the pages of the *New York Times*.

Divergence between crime rates and media coverage of crime was dramatic after 1994, when victimization declined much more precipitously than media attention to violent crime. Although there have been fewer stories about violent crime in the pages of the *New York Times* since its peak coverage of the subject in 1994, there are still almost twice as many stories about violent crime annually as there were before 1981. Compared to local news, especially local television news (Sacco 1995; Welch, Weber, and Edwards 2000; Pollak and Kubrin 2007), the *New York Times* offers a conservative version of the media's obsession with crime. But even reading one of America's leading newspapers might lead one to believe that violent crime has doubled over the past thirty years, when it has actually declined significantly by any measure and been cut in half according to the most reliable measure of violent crime: the murder rate. To be sure, different measures of crime and victimization have risen and fallen at different rates and to different levels over the past few decades. Property crime has fallen consistently since 1975, violent victimization exhibited steep declines after 1994, violent crimes reported to the police declined precipitously after 1993, and even the murder rate, which peaked in 1980, has been on the decline since 1991.

There is some debate about the best way to measure trends in crime (see, for example, Lynch and Biderman 1991; Lynch and Addington 2007). Even the nation's most reliable measure of crime, the National Crime Victimization Survey (NCVS), uses a household-based survey, so it probably does not adequately measure the experiences of marginalized populations. And since the NCVS does not ask inmates about their victimization experience, we may not be getting an adequate picture of trends over time. Despite all of these limitations, indications are that crime is down significantly from its peak by any measure. The four panels of figure 3.2 show trends over time in four leading indicators of crime and victimization. The murder rate, violent crimes reported to the police, and measures of violent victimization and property crime reported in victimization surveys all generate the same fundamental conclusion. Despite some discrepancies in the time series across measures, the trend over the last thirty years is unmistakable. Indeed, there were crime surges by most measures in the early 1980s and 1990s, but all measures of crime are down from their historic heights. What is even more puzzling is that, despite the recent economic downturn, crime rates continue to be at historic lows (see Rosenfeld 2009; Rosenfeld and Messner 2009).

Many studies have examined how local media attention to crime influences perceptions of crime and fear of victimization (for a review, see Surette 1998). Studies suggest that media portrayals of crime are significantly related to fear of crime, but that the effects are particularly salient for those whose risk of victimization is low, especially women, the elderly, and whites (Liska and Baccaglini 1990; Chiricos, Eschholz, and Gertz 1997). Although explanations for mass incarceration are complex and multifaceted, research has convincingly demonstrated a significant disconnect between crime rates and incarceration rates (see, for example, Mauer 2006), and studies have linked fear of crime to punitive attitudes in the criminal justice system (Dowler 2003; Sprott and Doob 1997).

Media attention to crime and victimization also shapes political stances about crime and criminal justice. When Illinois governor James Thompson (1982, 867) wrote, "No responsible public official is pro-crime," he might have said that no public official would like to be viewed as "soft on crime." Little did he know that being viewed as soft on crime would help to unravel Michael Dukakis's presidential campaign in 1988. While Dukakis was governor of Massachusetts, he supported a furlough program that granted inmates reprieves from their time in prison, ostensibly to aid their reintegration into society. One such inmate, William Horton, was charged and eventually convicted of robbery, rape, assault, and murder that occurred while he was on a furlough from prison. Dukakis's opponent in the 1988 presidential race, George H. W. Bush, suggested that Dukakis's support for the Massachusetts inmate furlough program indicated that he was soft on crime. Although it was unclear whether or to what extent this issue derailed Dukakis's campaign, it certainly was a lesson for other would-be politicians to avoid even the perception of being viewed as soft on crime. Michelle Alexander (2010) cogently explains how other politicians, perhaps less well known for their "tough on crime" stances, sponsored legislation and supported programs characterized by growing punitiveness.

Growing punitiveness, fueled by federal support for prison growth, increased surveillance, more aggressive policing and prosecution, and longer and more certain custodial sentences, has led to a massive increase in the size of the prison and jail population in the United States. Even as crime rates have fallen, the size of the penal population has increased (Mauer 2006). The number of inmates in America's prisons and jails more than quadrupled from 1980 to 2008. By the time of Barack Obama's inauguration, the Bureau of Justice Statistics (U.S. Department of Justice 2010) estimated that well over 2.3 million Americans were in prison or jail and that an additional 5 million were under criminal justice supervision, either through parole or probation.

Decades of growth in the criminal justice system coincided with a shift from a rehabilitative to a punitive philosophy within prisons and jails. Amer-

Figure 3.2   Trends in Crime Using Four Leading Indicators,
              1973 to 2008

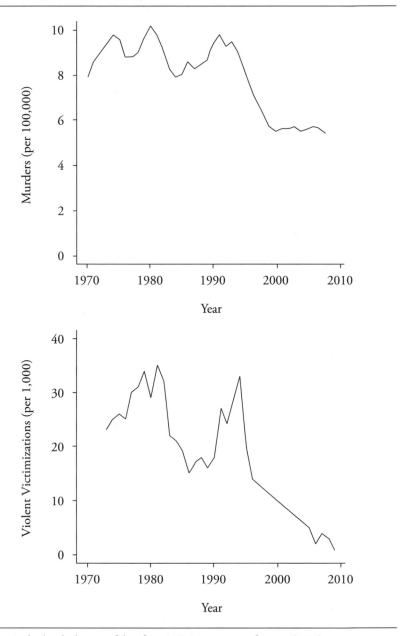

Source: Author's calculations of data from U.S. Department of Justice (2009).

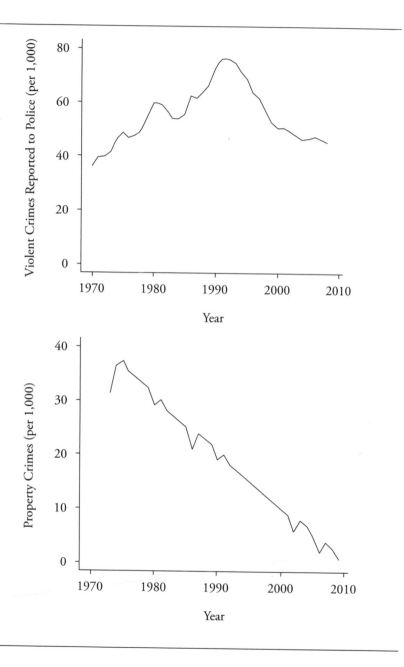

ica's prisons and jails offer few opportunities for inmates to gain the skills necessary to compete in an increasingly technical and global economy. As prison and jail counts have increased, correctional budgets are increasingly devoted to housing and surveilling inmates, with few resources remaining for rehabilitation programs within correctional facilities. By 2007, 6.8 percent of state general funds budgets were devoted to criminal justice (Pew Research Center on the States 2008). Yet, across the country, continuing education, preventative health care, and job training within prisons and jails have been drastically curtailed or eliminated. Data from the Bureau of Justice Statistics show that a declining fraction of inmates in any type of facility participate in education or training programs while incarcerated (U.S. Department of Justice 2003). Evidence suggests that the current generation of inmates, more than any other in the era of mass incarceration, is poorly equipped for self-sufficiency in the modern economy (Western 2006; Pager 2007). With low levels of education and little work experience in the formal economy, many of today's inmates face particularly bleak employment prospects after release.

Fiscal constraints, as well as emerging questions about whether continued prison growth generates public safety gains commensurate with its cost (Donohue 2009), coincided in 2009 with the first nationwide decline in the size of the U.S. prison population since 1971. There is evidence that the immigration detention system continues to expand, however, and represents the fastest-growing segment of the prison-industrial complex (Sabol, West, and Cooper 2009; Bosworth and Kaufman 2011; Minton 2010). Even before the modest nationwide decline in inmates was posted, several states, including California and New York, found themselves with too many inmates to house. California was mandated to reduce the prison population in order to provide adequate health care and ensure the safety of its inmates (Plata/Coleman vs. Schwarznegger, CV-01-01341, 2010).

Efforts to manage prison overcrowding and insufficient services for inmates have led to blanket releases, early parole, and the increased use of diversionary sentences like drug treatment or community supervision in lieu of a custodial sentence. Debates about the merits of continually increasing spending on correctional populations have reached a fevered pitch, especially with the negative impacts of the recent economic downturns on state revenues and budgets. States all across the country have wrestled with balanced budget mandates and budget-cutting proposals. For the first time in decades, states and local governments have stopped plans to build new prisons. Only time will tell if 2008 marked the zenith of America's experiment in mass incarceration.

The expense of managing America's prisons and jails has continued to escalate because of aging facilities, an aging and increasingly disadvantaged prison and jail population, and the intensification of surveillance activities within correctional facilities. Although the data are hard to find, many analysts suspect that we have been investing growing fractions of correctional budgets in housing and surveilling inmates. The development of "supermax" prisons marks a relatively recent trend toward heightened surveillance and extended control over inmates (Riveland 1999). It is unclear exactly how many inmates are housed in supermax prisons or supermax units within other facilities across the country, but data show that over 40 percent of federal inmates are in medium- and maximum-security facilities. In 2009, 11 percent of federal prisoners were housed in high-security prisons, and another 29.8 percent were housed in medium-security prisons (U.S. Department of Justice 2009).

Supermax prisons or supermax units within prisons represent the extreme of criminal justice surveillance. They are typically characterized by a high level of control over and surveillance of inmates. Inmates in supermax facilities are often bereft of human contact, yet they are constantly surveilled through video and electronic technology (Rhodes 2004). In her book *Total Confinement* (2004), Lorna Rhodes describes in elaborate detail the daily routines of inmates living in a supermax prison and the implications of isolation and constant surveillance for the psychological well-being of inmates. The isolation and intensive supervision found in supermax prisons exacerbates existing psychological illnesses in some inmates and triggers acute deviant behavior in others (Rhodes 2004). Inmates in supermax settings are arguably the most intensively surveilled, yet at the same time the most acutely marginalized, of all of America's inmates.

Yet even in other prisons with lower levels of security, inmates are tightly controlled and repeatedly counted. Hourly head-counts are commonplace in overcrowded prisons, where prison guards count and log the number of inmates throughout the day and night. Inmates are also counted before and after routine activities like meals, before and after moving between units, and at specified and sometimes impromptu intervals. Probationers and parolees are also actively monitored. Geographic restrictions on probationers and parolees are a unique form of social control (Beckett and Herbert 2009). Electronic monitoring systems, ankle bracelets, and periodic check-ins with parole officers are defining features of contemporary criminal justice supervision. In some jurisdictions, a parolee can be readmitted to prison for failing to update his or her address with a parole officer, and missing an appointment with a parole officer is a violation worthy of prison readmission. In many jurisdictions, permission from a parole officer is required for parolees to travel across county or state lines; some parolees face blanket prohibitions against interstate travel.

THE EXCLUSION OF INMATES

There is a deep and fundamental irony in the exclusion of inmates. States and localities are keen to know exactly how many inmates there are, and urban and rural communities alike vie to include prison and jail residents in local population totals. Private prison facilities are reimbursed based on services provided to inmates, and so they carefully record and report the number of inmates in their care. In 2006, *Business Week* featured an article suggesting that private prison companies were a safe stock buy because they had the capacity to handle excess prison population from overcrowded state prisons (Ghosh 2006).

Debates over how and where inmates count are especially pitched when determining the allocation of congressional seats associated with Census counts. At the federal level, allocation of seats in the U.S. House of Representatives is based solely on Census enumerations; for those purposes, inmates count where they reside. That is, inmates are counted within the state where the correctional facility is located.

At the state level, there is no prohibition against adjusting Census estimates or collecting additional data when determining political representation or other allocative decisions within states (Mahan v. Howell, 410 U.S. 315, 330–32, 1973). Research by the Prison Policy Initiative finds that states and localities commonly "adjust" Census estimates regarding the distribution of military personnel, students, and inmates (Wagner et al. 2010). New York recently passed statewide legislation to adjust Census counts to include inmates where they resided before they were incarcerated instead of counting inmates where they currently reside in prison or jail. Seven other states have legislation pending (Wagner et al. 2010).

The Bureau of Justice Statistics is tasked with compiling data on the number and composition of the inmate population. Self-proclaimed as "the United States' primary source for criminal justice statistics," the Bureau of Justice Statistics was first established in 1979 as the result of an amendment to the Omnibus Crime Control and Safe Streets Act of 1968. The agency's mission is to "collect, analyze, publish, and disseminate information on crime, criminal offenders, victims of crime, and the operation of justice systems at all levels of government. These data are critical to federal, state, and local policymakers in combating crime and ensuring that justice is both efficient and evenhanded" (U.S. Department of Justice 2010).

For the purposes of most federal policy construction and nearly all social scientific research that is not directly related to crime or criminal justice, inmates are rarely considered. Institutionalization in correctional facilities severs people from most federally administered data collection efforts. Inmates are not included in surveys that use probability-based samples drawn from households. Federal statistical agencies other than the Bureau of Justice Statistics collect surprisingly little information about inmates and almost none of it directly from inmates. Even the Census does an admittedly poor job of counting inmates (Citro et al. 2004). The first iteration of the American Community Survey in 2005, which was intended to replace the long form of the Census, did not survey individuals living in institutions. Later iterations formally include incarcerated individuals, but evidence suggests that the American Community Survey has not effectively counted inmates. Although the rules for enumerating inmates are clear, there is evidence that the Census Bureau routinely undercounts inmates and does a poor job of collecting detailed information about their characteristics, needs, or capacities. In recognition of this shortcoming, in early 2010, in advance of the decennial Census, the Census Bureau actively sought to recruit ethnographers to investigate the conduct of the Census in prison and jail facilities around the country (Laura Rhodes, personal communication, 2010; Michelle Interbitzen, personal communication, 2010).

Today crime and justice loom large in the public psyche, and inmates are carefully surveilled when under criminal justice supervision, yet inmates are poorly enumerated in federal data collection efforts save those directly related to the criminal justice system. Moreover, little information of relevance is collected from them. In fact, there are significant discrepancies in federally provided data sources about the exact size and composition of the inmate population. All of this contributes to the invisibility of large segments of certain sociodemographic groups.

Perhaps even more puzzling is that federally provided data sources generate wildly differing estimates of the fraction of young, black, low-skill men in prison or jail on any given day. The discrepancy has less to do with how to count inmates and more to do with how to estimate the educational distribution of the population (for more on this, see chapter 4). The size of the inmate population has become so large, and incarceration so disproportionately concentrated among young, low-skill black men, that it distorts federal statistics on the educational distribution of the wider population. To foreshadow the results reported in chapter 4, the American Community Survey estimates that close to 10 percent of young black men are high school dropouts, the Current Population Survey estimates 13 percent, and combining CPS data with data on inmates suggests that the figure is closer to 20 percent.

Disparate estimates of the high school dropout rate among young black men also leads to sharply contrasting estimates of the fraction of low-skill black men who are incarcerated. Table 3.1 shows five alternative estimates of the fraction of black and white low-skill men incarcerated in America's prisons and jails to illustrate how assumptions about the educational distribution affect incarceration rates within education groups. In 1980, when incarceration was relatively rare, the incarceration rate ranged between 1.9 and 2.4 percent among young white male dropouts and between 8.2 and 10.6 percent among young black dropouts. The incarceration rate among young white men is relatively insensitive to different measures of the educational distribution because the fraction of the population incarcerated is small relative to the group size. Among black men, however, the incarceration rate is highly sensitive to assumptions about the educational distribution of the group because the number of men incarcerated is large relative to the size of the group.

By 2008, as the prison and jail population swelled, the variability in the measurement of incarceration increased for both groups, but dramatically so among low-skill black men. Estimates presented in table 3.1 suggest that the fraction of young, low-skill, black men incarcerated ranged from 29.6 to 54.8 percent. The lowest estimate, derived exclusively from American Community Survey data on the proportion of the group that was institutionalized, is likely to be far too low. Exactly why the Census Bureau does a poor job of

Table 3.1   Incarceration Rates of Men Ages Twenty to Thirty-Four
             with Less Than a High School Education, 1980 to 2008

	1980		2008	
Data Source	Non-Hispanic White	Non-Hispanic Black	Non-Hispanic White	Non-Hispanic Black
Census institutionalized	3.5%	9.6%	8.3%[a]	29.6%[a]
Census corrections	2.0	8.2	—	—
Census education	1.9	9.0	14.2	48.8
CPS education	2.2	9.9	13.3	51.9
CPS adjusted education	2.1	9.4	11.9	36.8
Civilian	2.4	10.6	12.0	37.2

Source: Author's calculations. See the methodological appendix for more details.
[a] Represents estimates for 2007, the latest year for which data were available.

enumerating young, black, low-skill men in prison and jail is a question for Census ethnographers. The highest estimate, using information from the Census on the educational distribution of the population, is likely to be far too high. The undercount of individuals with low levels of education in the non-institutionalized population may contribute to inflated estimates of the fraction of low-skill men incarcerated.

The other estimates shown in the table use data from the Bureau of Justice Statistics on inmate counts combined with population estimates provided by the Census Bureau or generated by data from the Current Population Survey. Data from both the Census Bureau and the Current Population Survey make the population seem more educated than it is, particularly within sociodemographic groups with high incarceration rates (see chapter 4). The fifth row of the table "adjusts" educational distributions generated from the CPS to include those living in prisons and jails. This method generates results almost identical to the civilian incarceration rates shown in the sixth row, where CPS data are adjusted to include inmates.

In summary, table 3.1 illustrates one of the fundamental problems that plagues the research and policymaking surrounding America's most disadvantaged groups. Many socially marginalized individuals elude the census-taker and the survey researcher. Their exclusion from our data collection efforts leaves a great deal of uncertainty not only about their numbers but also about their experience. The remaining chapters of this book attempt to shed light on the implications of their exclusion for the measurement of black progress.

CONCLUSION

This chapter sought to unveil the contradiction between the visibility of crime and incarceration and the invisibility of inmates and former inmates. America is a culture fascinated by crime and criminality, and the pages of national and local newspapers commonly lead with stories about crime and violence. There has been growing media attention to violent crime even as declines in crime rates are obvious by any measure of crime or victimization. Would-be criminals, inmates, probationers, and parolees are vigilantly surveilled. Police cameras have become ubiquitous in America's cities. Although there is little evidence that video surveillance deters would-be criminals, cameras have become de rigueur at crime "hot spots" in large and small cities alike. In supermax prisons and community supervision programs, modern technology is used to surveil and control would-be deviants.

Yet even in an environment of heightened sensitivity to crime and near-constant surveillance of those involved in the criminal justice system, inmates and former inmates often evade inclusion in the data collection efforts used in social policy formulation and evaluation and social science research. The Census commonly overlooks them, and sample surveys of individuals living in households exclude them. In addition, the federal government does not systematically collect data on inmates' community of origin or information about where inmates plan to live after release from prison or jail. Only through careful fieldwork or piecing together information from surveys of the institutionalized population with information from other sources can we identify the experiences of individuals and social and demographic groups who have spent time in America's prisons and jails.

This is not the first time research methods have not kept pace with changing American lifestyles. For example, although cohabitation prior to, or in lieu of, marriage has been common in the United States for decades, we have only recently begun collecting data in a systematic way that allows researchers and policymakers to develop a detailed understanding of the lived experience of unmarried cohabitors. Similarly, while many Americans identify as "mixed-race" individuals, individuals continue to be asked to choose only one race category on most federally administered surveys. The Census itself is an exception since 2000, when it allowed individuals to choose more than one race.

Although America's prisons and jails have been expanding for over thirty-five years, our research designs continue to overlook the most disadvantaged segments of the population housed in them. The consequences of those omissions for the estimation of economic, political, and social inequalities are the focus of the remainder of this book.

CHAPTER 4

Illusions of Progress

> It is our position that any legislative or governmental classification must fall with an even hand on all persons similarly situated.
> —Robert Carter, oral argument before the U.S. Supreme Court in Brown v. Board of Education of Topeka, Kansas (1952)

Steep racial and class disparities in incarceration have produced a generation of social outliers whose collective experience is wholly different from that of the rest of American society. The extreme concentration of incarceration rates in certain sociodemographic groups is compounded by the obviously segregative function of the penal system, which often relocates people to far-flung facilities distant from their communities and families. As a result, people in prison and jail are disconnected from the basic institutions—households and the labor market—that dominate our common understanding and measurement of the general population. The segregation and social concentration of incarceration thus help conceal its effects. This fact is particularly important for public policy because in assessing the social and economic well-being of the population, the incarcerated fraction is frequently overlooked and racial inequality is underestimated as a result.

This idea can be illustrated by considering educational and economic outcomes. For example, more than fifty years after Brown v. Board of Education, blacks still lag behind whites in high school graduation rates. Yet the exact size of the racial gap in high school completion and recent trends in the size of the race gap are debated. In 2006 the *Washington Post* featured a series of articles

Figure 4.1   High School Dropout Rates for Men Ages Twenty to Thirty-Four, 1980 to 2008

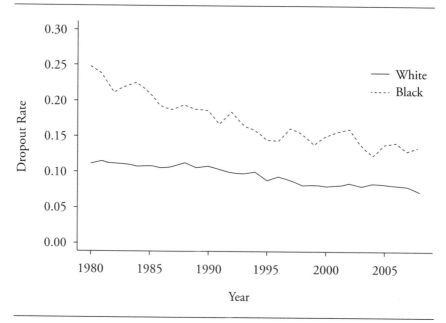

Source: Author's calculations using data from the March Current Population Survey (U.S. Census Bureau, various years). See methodological appendix for more details.

and commentaries that discussed how different data and measures generate a high school completion rate that ranges between 70 and 82 percent (Mathews 2006; Mishel and Roy 2006; Greene and Winters 2006); this is a remarkable discrepancy for such a common statistic with important implications for public policy and sociological conceptions of the production and maintenance of inequality.

Writing in the early 2000s, Rebecca Blank (2001, 26) observed that "high school completion continues to inch up among both Whites and Blacks, with substantially greater progress among Blacks; so that the White-Black high school dropout rates are slowly converging over time." Consistent with this claim, data from the Current Population Survey, shown in figure 4.1, suggest steady declines in the proportion of African American men who fail to complete high school either through school completion or equivalency degrees over the past three decades. Adam Gamoran (2001) concluded that black and white high school completion rates had approached parity by the end of the

1990s, and he predicted a decline in racial inequality across other measures of attainment such as college enrollment and completion throughout the twenty-first century.

Another strand of research contends that graduation rates of white and minority students have not converged as is commonly thought (Heckman and LaFontaine 2010; Greene 2002; Orfield et al. 2004). For example, Common Core of Data (CCD) collects data on public elementary and secondary schools obtained from the administrative records of state education agencies, with annual statistical data collected on approximately 18,000 public school districts covering approximately 100,000 public elementary and secondary schools. Data are used to compute national dropout rates. These data indicate substantially higher rates of high school dropout and recent increases in high school dropout rates, especially among African Americans (Warren and Halpern-Manners 2009; Heckman and LaFontaine 2010). After a careful review and analysis of a number of data sources, James Heckman and Paul LaFontaine (2010, 3) observe no evidence of convergence in minority-majority graduation rates over the past thirty-five years.

Surveys commonly used to gauge the educational attainment of the population, including the Current Population Survey, use a sampling frame that draws respondents from persons living in households. A non-institutionalized, household-based sample categorically excludes people housed in institutions, including people in the military and in prison. While researchers have noted the potential importance of this sample bias, few have investigated the issue in greater detail (see Heckman and LaFontaine 2010; Warren and Halpern-Manners 2009; Mishel and Roy 2006). Heckman and LaFontaine (2010) conclude that the exclusion of the military population does not affect estimates of high school graduation given the small proportion of the population who are enlisted. Although the exclusion of prison and jail inmates has little effect on the measurement of overall U.S. graduation rates, they note, the exclusion of prison and jail inmates from CPS data is consequential for estimating race and gender gaps in graduation rates (Heckman and LaFontaine 2010). Failing to include inmates in estimates of educational attainment not only underestimates the extent of racial inequality in high school graduation but also obscures the role that educational institutions play in the production and maintenance of social inequality.

Incarceration also has an impact on our assessment of employment rates as they are conventionally measured by the Current Population Survey. For groups that are weakly attached to the labor market, like young men with little education, economic status is often measured by the employment-to-population ratio (see, for example, Welch 1990). This figure, more expansive than the unemployment rate, counts as jobless those who have dropped out of the labor market altogether (that is, who are not currently looking for work). Again, however, because the Current Population Survey is restricted to those living in households, the institutionalized are not included in the survey-based description of the population. Even though some inmates work while in prison or jail, for all policy purposes, they are not considered to be engaged in the formal economy; the employment of inmates is not subject to minimum wage laws, collective bargaining agreements, or unemployment insurance. By ignoring inmates, we underestimate labor inactivity.

Economic inequality between black and white men is often measured by wage differences in the civilian labor force (see, for example, Cancio, Evans, and Maume 1996; Sakamoto, Wu, and Tzeng 2000; McCall 2001; Grodsky and Pager 2001). However, comparisons of wage-earners may inaccurately describe the relative economic status of black men if there are strong race differences in labor force attachment or changes in employment over time. Because the jobless rate is high among men with low potential earnings, relatively few low-skill black men are included in assessments of wage inequality. The lower tail of the black wage distribution is further truncated by the joblessness of inmates. As the criminal justice system has grown, the observed wages of black men increasingly overstate the economic well-being of the general population. Moreover, reliance on estimates of the population derived from household-based samples increasingly understate racial inequality in economic outcomes.

High school graduation is an important indicator of social and economic status. Similarly, group-level employment rates and cumulative wages are commonly used to indicate the relative economic status of different social and demographic groups. Three decades ago, William Darity (1980) argued that the exclusion of the unemployed population from estimates of wages overstated the relative economic standing of blacks and created an illusion of black economic progress. This chapter explores how the exclusion of prison and jail inmates from the calculation of educational attainment, the employment-to-population ratio, and the racial wage gap influence the measurement of fundamental educational and economic indicators, and to what extent the true educational and economic standing of black men is thereby obscured.

INCARCERATION IN THE LAND
OF OPPORTUNITY

America is often characterized as a land of opportunity, and overwhelming majorities of Americans continue to believe that individuals determine their own economic success (Pew Economic Mobility Project 2009, 9). Education is commonly viewed as a key path to economic mobility. According to a recent study, over 80 percent of survey respondents report that "having a good education," as well as "having ambition," "hard work," and "staying healthy," is important to an individual's economic mobility (Pew Economic Mobility Project 2009).

America's opportunity structure, however, has long advantaged the rights of some groups over others (Fischer et al. 1996). Slavery, Jim Crow laws, and segregation restricted the rights and opportunities of African Americans. Numerous judicial decisions in the 1950s and the civil rights legislation of the 1960s promised a new era of opportunity for America's blacks through increased education and employment opportunities. Yet a growing chorus laments the slow progress of American blacks over the past fifty years, and there is a growing contention that the criminal justice system maintains racial inequality in the United States (Alexander 2010; Wacquant 2000, 2001; Western 2006).

The expansion of higher education in the United States after World War II has been linked to widening educational opportunities and increased social mobility through educational attainment (Blau and Duncan 1967; Raftery and Hout 1993). Educational expansion is thought to enhance the educational chances of even formerly disadvantaged classes, thus providing a path to upward mobility (Raftery and Hout 1993). As more educational opportunities become available, more students, including those from disadvantaged backgrounds, are able to pursue further education. Numerous studies have found evidence of the mobility-enhancing effects of educational expansion in the United States and other countries (Hanley 2001; Shavit and Blossfeld 1993; Hout, Raftery, and Bell 1993).

Data from the Current Population Survey are consistent with the claim that educational expansion has fueled declines in racial inequality in education. The educational attainment measure on the March CPS indicates whether an individual has failed to complete high school or acquire a general equivalency degree (GED). Although this is technically not a measure of high school dropout, the CPS measure of high school or GED completion is commonly used to track trends in educational attainment over time. Throughout this book, unless otherwise noted, "high school dropout" is used synonymously with failure to complete high school or acquire a GED.

Reliance on data from the Current Population Survey might lead one to believe that the high school dropout rate has fallen precipitously and that racial inequality has narrowed during the period of penal expansion. For example, in 1980, 11.2 percent of non-Hispanic white men between the ages of twenty and thirty-four had not completed high school or a GED. By 2008, the number of high school dropouts in this group had fallen to 7.2 percent. Among non-Hispanic black men in the same age group, the high school dropout rate fell from 24.8 percent to 13.5 percent over the same period, resulting in a 45 percent decline in the dropout rate among young black men and a 53 percent decline in the black-white gap in high school completion over the period.

Apart from the effects of mass incarceration on educational parity, there is evidence that schools themselves sow the seeds of inequality. Schools socialize and prepare students to assume their position in the class structure through a variety of mechanisms (Bowles and Gintis 1976; Willis 1977; Lucas 2001; Lareau 2003; Kozol 1991). Early work by Samuel Bowles and Herbert Gintis (1976) and Paul Willis (1977) contended that schools reflect the occupational structure and expectations found in society. Annette Lareau (2003) has recently extended this paradigm to examine how the parenting styles of middle- and working-class families intersect with the educational system to engender educational inequalities. By teaching their children how to interact and reason with authority figures, middle-class parents instill and reinforce skills that provide the foundation for future success. Teachers and individuals in positions of authority and power later reward or devalue these reasoning and interactional skills. In an increasingly technical and knowledge-based economy, the skills learned by middle-class children are most often rewarded while those of the working class are devalued.

Samuel Lucas's (1999, 2001) work emphasizes how tracking systems reinforce social inequality by establishing qualitative distinctions within high schools. Although tracking practices purport to assign students to instructional groups based on ability, assignment is not usually based solely on actual ability level (Hallinan 1994; Page 1991). Rather, tracking segregates students by social and economic characteristics in such a way that low-income and minority students are disproportionately assigned to lower tracks (Gamoran et al. 1995; Hallinan 1994). Students placed in low-ability groups then receive an inferior quantity and quality of instruction compared to those in higher-track groups (Gamoran et al. 1995; Hallinan 1994). Therefore, tracking enables socioeconomically advantaged students to secure a qualitatively better education (Lucas 2001).

Inequalities in school funding have been key to explaining how schools concentrate disadvantage and reproduce inequality. Jonathan Kozol (1991) has documented the "savage inequalities" between inner-city schools, attended primarily by low-income minorities, and more affluent suburban schools, examining differences in per pupil expenditures, available resources, and experience levels of teachers. He contends that underresourced schools in poor urban areas leave the students who attend them ill prepared to pursue higher education or high-wage jobs.

Consistent with sociological ideas that the educational system reproduces inequality through a variety of mechanisms, including socialization processes, tracking, and funding levels, a variety of organizations have drawn attention to the concept of a "school-to-prison" pipeline. The American Civil Liberties Union (ACLU) labels it one of the most pressing civil rights issues of the day, and the National Association for the Advancement of Colored People (NAACP) has made it a focus of its attention (NAACP Legal Defense and Education Fund 2007). Critics argue that zero-tolerance suspensions, expulsions, metal detectors, and near-constant surveillance better prepare already disadvantaged youth for a career in the criminal justice system than for one productively engaged in the paid labor force.

The siphoning effects of the criminal justice system obscure the extent of educational disadvantage faced by those most at risk of spending time in prison or jail. While socioeconomically advantaged students benefit from segregated educational systems to secure more successful educational outcomes, those same mechanisms impede the academic success of socioeconomically disadvantaged and minority students by limiting the quality and quantity of the education they receive. Educational attainment has important implications for inequalities in a number of domains, including occupational attainment, income, childbearing, health, the likelihood of receiving public assistance, and the likelihood of contact with the criminal justice system (Swanson and Chaplin 2003; Warren and Halpern-Manners 2009; Child Trends 2003). But the extent of those inequalities is obscured because the criminal justice system, a repository for America's most disadvantaged, effectively hides them from view.

High incarceration rates characterize particular sociodemographic groups, and inmates, now more than ever, are defined by having low levels of education. There is a strong and durable link between educational attainment and contact with the criminal justice system. Decades of criminological research have established a link between education, employment opportunities, and criminal involvement (Lochner and Moretti 2004; Crutchfield and Pitchford 1997; Crutchfield 1989). Research has documented the growing concentration of incarceration among high school dropouts (Pettit and Western 2004; Western 2006).

Public investments in education are also thought to influence criminal justice contact. Richard Arum and Gary LaFree (2008) show that increased investments in educational resources at the state level, measured as student-teacher ratios, are associated with lower risks of incarceration. They find a similar negative relationship between educational resources and the likelihood of incarceration at the school level. Arum and Irenee Beattie (1999) argue that investments in education can decrease the long-term costs of adult imprisonment.

There is a growing contention that the education-incarceration link has been fueled by increased state spending on corrections while spending on education has lagged (Pew Research Center on the States 2008). When state governments increase spending on corrections, their obligation to meet balanced-budget mandates often leaves less money available for other priorities, including the very educational opportunities that might stem the flow of disadvantaged children through the school-to-prison pipeline.

Decades of prison growth coupled with high concentrations of incarceration among low-skill black men have important consequences for the measurement of racial inequalities in educational attainment as well as employment and wage outcomes. To the extent that educational attainment is a key determinant of economic opportunities and outcomes, the exclusion of inmates from measures of economic standing will lead to a fundamental distortion of over-time trends of black economic progress.

EDUCATION

Although incarceration in prison and jail used to be reserved primarily for violent and repeat offenders, incarceration is now common among nonvio-

Table 4.1   Demographic Characteristics of Inmates in Local, State, and Federal Correctional Facilities, 1980 and 2008

	1980	2008
Male	94.7%	91.5%
Age in years	29.4	34.3
Non-Hispanic white	42.9%	35.0%
Non-Hispanic black	42.5	41.4
Hispanic	12.3	18.7
Other race	2.2	4.8
Less than high school	51.0	55.7
High school/GED	34.6	31.4
Some college	14.4	12.9

Source: Author's calculations. See the methodological appendix for more details.

lent property and drug offenders. High rates of incarceration have become a social fact among young, low-skill, black men. As documented in chapters 1 and 2, well over one-third of young black men who do not finish high school are in prison or jail on any given day, and almost 70 percent of black male dropouts are imprisoned at some point during their lives.

Table 4.1 illustrates the changing demographics of inmates by comparing inmate characteristics in 1980 and 2008. In 1980 the prison and jail population was 94.7 percent male and had a mean age of 29.4 years. Although blacks were significantly overrepresented in the prison and jail population relative to their proportion of the general population, there were slightly more whites than blacks behind bars in the early years of criminal justice expansion. Just over half of all inmates had less than a high school diploma. By 2008, the incarcerated population included more women and the mean age of inmates was nearly five years higher than in 1980. African Americans represented the largest share of inmates, though Hispanics saw sizable increases in their share of the incarcerated population over the period since 1980. Perhaps most striking is that while conventional wisdom suggests that the educational levels of the non-institutionalized population saw significant increases after 1980, inmates were on average less well educated in 2008 than in 1980. By 2008, 55.7 percent of all inmates had less than a high school diploma.

Figure 4.2   Adjusted High School Dropout Rates for Men Ages Twenty to Thirty-Four, 1980 to 2008

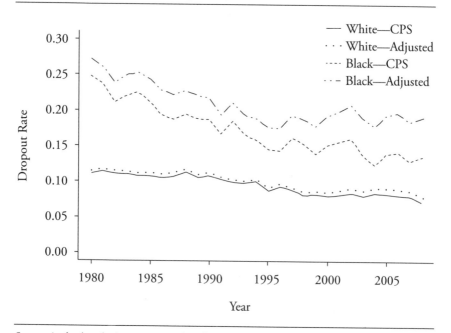

Source: Author's calculations using data from the March Current Population Survey (U.S. Census Bureau, various years) and data from the Bureau of Justice Statistics Surveys of Inmates (U.S. Dept. of Justice, BJS, various years–a, various years–b, various years–c). See the methodological appendix for more details.

In 2008, 52.7 percent of white and 61.8 percent of black male inmates between the ages of twenty and thirty-four had dropped out of high school and had not received a GED. These numbers dwarf the rates of high school failure in the non-institutionalized population as estimated by the Current Population Survey, and they confirm the extent of educational disadvantage among the inmate population. Overall, inmates of all racial and ethnic groups drop out of high school at high levels, but the high school dropout rates are substantially higher among incarcerated black men than white men.

Figure 4.2 shows high school dropout rates estimated using the Current Population Survey and adjusted dropout rates that include information about the prison and jail population. The figure shows four lines. The solid (lowest) line shows the dropout rate among white men ages twenty to thirty-four from 1980 through 2008. The line shows a small but steady decrease in the fraction of this population who did not complete high school or an equivalency degree. The dotted line just above the solid line is the dropout rate adjusted to include inmates. The two top lines show the same statistic for black men ages twenty to thirty-four; the lower dashed line reflects the observed dropout rate using data from the CPS, and the top line includes inmates.

Low levels of educational attainment among prison and jail inmates lead to higher adjusted dropout rates for both whites and blacks than conventional statistics using the Current Population Survey would imply. In other words, measures of the high school graduation rate that exclude inmates consistently underestimate high school dropout or overestimate the educational attainment of the U.S. population.

The effect of excluding inmates on estimates of graduation rates has grown over time as the prison and jail population has expanded. In 1980 the exclusion of inmates from estimates of the high school dropout rate led to a 2.7 percent difference in the estimate of high school dropout rates for young white men and a 9.3 percent difference for young black men. By 2008, conventional data sources that exclude the incarcerated population underestimated the dropout rate among young white men by 11 percent. Among young black men, the dropout rate was underestimated by 40 percent.

Differences in the size of the adjustment over time and by race suggest that conventional data sources that exclude the incarcerated population underestimate not only the high school dropout rate but also racial inequality in educational outcomes. Data from the Current Population Survey imply that the black-white gap in high school completion, through either formal schooling or a GED, narrowed from 13.6 to 6.3 percentage points between 1980 and 2008. Including inmates, we find little improvement in the black-white gap in high school for the last twenty years. Figure 4.3 shows that including inmates suggests that the racial gap in high school completion among men has hovered close to its current level of 11 percentage points for most of the past twenty years.

Penal system growth has contributed to large, growing, and statistically significant adjustments to estimates of racial inequality in the high school dropout rate. In recent years, the race differences in dropout rates estimated using solely the Current Population Survey and those that include inmates have been as large as 110 percent (for more detail, see Ewert, Pettit, and Sykes 2010). In 2008, including inmates in estimates suggested that the racial gap in the high school dropout rate among young men was 11 percent, or 4.7 per-

Figure 4.3   Racial Inequality in High School Dropout Rates of Men
              Ages Twenty to Thirty-Four, 1980 to 2008

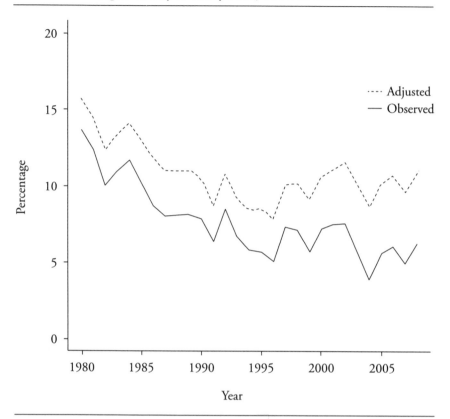

Source: Author's calculations using data from the March Current Population Survey (U.S. Census Bureau, various years) and data from the Bureau of Justice Statistics Surveys of Inmates (U.S. Dept. of Justice, BJS, various years–a, various years–b, various years–c). See the methodological appendix for more details.

centage points higher than the estimate of 6.3 percent derived from the non-institutionalized population in the Current Population Survey. Reliance on the Current Population Survey underestimates racial inequality in the high school dropout rate in 2008 by 75 percent.

EMPLOYMENT

Between 1980 and 2008, the percentage of white men of working age employed in the paid labor force ranged from 78 to 84 percent, rising and falling

Figure 4.4   Employment-Population Ratios for Men Ages Twenty to
Thirty-Four with Less Than a High School Degree, 1980
to 2008

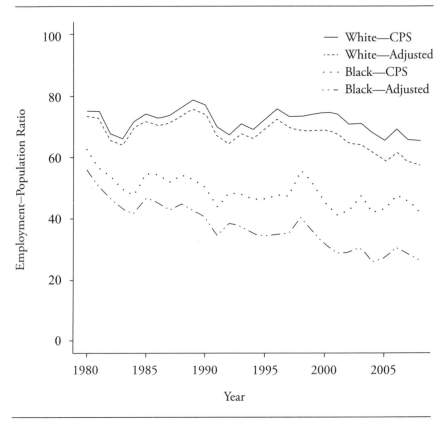

Source: Author's calculations of data from Pettit, Sykes, and Western (2009).

with overall employment rates and economic cycles. Employment rates were consistently 12 to 16 percent lower among black men, with the widest gaps occurring when the performance of the overall economy was particularly poor. Similar patterns in racial inequality are found for employment among young men between the ages of twenty and thirty-four, although conventional data sources indicate that employment rates of young men are generally a bit higher than those of men of all working ages.

Recent economic changes and technological shifts have coincided with particularly low employment rates among low-skill men. Data from the Current Population Survey, shown in figure 4.4, indicate that three-quarters of young, low-skill, white men were working in 1980. By 2008, that number had fallen to less than two-thirds (65 percent). Declines in employment among their black counterparts have been even sharper since 1980. The CPS reports that 62 percent of young, low-skill, black men were employed in 1980. Over the next twenty-eight years, that number fell by over 20 percentage points. Conventional data sources indicate that fewer than 42 percent of black male dropouts were employed on any given day in 2008.

As bleak as these numbers may seem, they tell only half the story. In fact, the employment prospects of young men are even worse than they at first appear. Owing to the disproportionate concentration of incarceration among low-skill men, the men with the poorest employment prospects are increasingly likely to be excluded from surveys used to generate trends in employment, like the Current Population Survey. Including inmates in estimates of employment-population ratios (also shown in figure 4.4) suggests that employment rates among young, black, low-skill men have fallen by more than half since 1980.

High rates of black joblessness are often traced to structural causes such as urban deindustrialization or the spatial segregation of minority neighborhoods (Wilson 1987; Kain 1971; Kasarda 1989; Massey and Denton 1993). In addition, three decades of escalating incarceration rates have severely reduced labor force participation among young African American men. Incarceration now rivals urban deindustrialization and spatial segregation as a key suspect in low employment rates among black men. By 2008, more than one-quarter of all jobless black men under age thirty-five were in prison or jail, compared to just 9 percent of young white men.

Table 4.2 shows the growing contribution of incarceration to joblessness. Among white men of working age, 2.4 percent of the jobless were in prison or jail in 1980 compared to 5.6 percent in 2008. The percentage of inmates among the jobless is now twice as high for young white men (9.6 percent compared with 4.2 percent in 1980). The share of the jobless in prison or jail is much higher for blacks. Almost 21 percent of jobless black men of working age were in prison or jail in 2008. Among young black men, incarceration accounted for 27.4 percent of all joblessness in the same year.

Including inmates in employment-population ratios suggests that conventional labor force statistics significantly overestimate the labor force involvement of African American men, and of young black men in particular. But the group most acutely affected is also the group with the highest incarcera-

Table 4.2   Percentage of Jobless in Prison or Jail, 1980 to 2008

	1980		2008	
	Non-Hispanic White	Non-Hispanic Black	Non-Hispanic White	Non-Hispanic Black
Eighteen to sixty-four	2.4%	9.6%	5.6%	20.8%
Twenty to thirty-four	4.2	16.7	9.2	27.4
Twenty to thirty-four with less than a high school degree	8.7	23.8	28.2	50.4

Source: Author's calculations. See the methodological appendix for more details.

tion rates: young black men with less than a high school diploma. As scholars and analysts were extolling improvements in the economic well-being of young blacks (Freeman and Rodgers 2000; Holzer and Offner 2006), more and more low-skill blacks were landing in prison or jail. By 2008, a young black man without a high school diploma was more likely to be in prison or jail than to be employed in the paid labor force. Employment-population rates adjusted to include inmates suggest that only 26 percent of young, black, male dropouts were employed in 2008, while over 37 percent were in prison or jail. Over half of the joblessness of young, black, male dropouts is linked to incarceration.

Although conventional data sources suggest that the employment rate of young blacks has generally kept pace with that of young whites, accounting for penal system growth suggests that the black-white employment gap is now significantly wider than it has been since 1980. Among all working-age men, the race gap in employment increased 16 percent between 1980 and 2008. Among young men, the gap increased 40 percent, from 16.1 percent to 22.5 percent. Among poorly educated men, the race gap in employment grew dramatically in the 1980s and even into the 1990s. By 2008, employment rates among young, black, low-skill men were less than half of those of similarly educated white men.

WAGES

The picture for wage inequality is slightly more complicated, but the impact of incarceration on the measurement of racial inequality in wages is similar to that found for education and employment. Conventional data sources indicate that the wage advantage of working-age whites changed little from 1985 to 2008. The hourly wage of white men between the ages of eighteen and sixty-five exceeded that of blacks by about 32 percent in 2008. Earnings inequality between whites and blacks increased from 1980 through 1985, declined through much of the 1990s and 2000s, then widened again by 2008.

Among young men, inequality increased much more dramatically compared to working-age men until the mid-1980s and then declined more dramatically through the 1990s and 2000s. The solid line in figure 4.5 shows that by 2008, conventional data suggest, the hourly wage of young white men exceeded that of blacks by just over 20 percent. The relative earnings of young black men were falling through the early 1980s (Bound and Freeman 1992, table 1; Cancio et al. 1996); observed wage inequality peaked in 1985 and then fell by about 20 percent over the next twenty-three years (figure 4.5).

But as we saw earlier in this chapter, incarceration contributes to growing joblessness, especially among low-skill black men. Increased joblessness due to incarceration drove up reports of average wages of blacks, inflating estimates of black economic progress. In fact, as the dashed and dotted lines in figure 4.5 indicate, including inmates in estimates of average wages suggests that racial inequality in average wages among young men has seen no improvement since the early 1990s. The dashed line assumes that inmates earn comparable wages to men of similar age (A) and education (E) observed in the labor force; it is thus labeled the age-education adjustment (AE-ADJ). The dotted line makes similar assumptions about wages by age and education and also assumes that inmates experience a wage penalty in proportion to their wages relative to similarly skilled men prior to incarceration (I); hence, it is labeled the age-education-incarceration adjustment (AEI-ADJ). In summary, even very conservative assumptions about the wage prospects of inmates, indicated by the age-education adjustment, suggest that data that exclude inmates significantly overestimate wage offers among black men because inmates are drawn disproportionately from the bottom of the wage distribution. Assumptions that take into account the relatively low wages of inmates prior to incarceration suggest even larger adjustments.

If we consider trends in average hourly wages that include the unemployed, the picture is even bleaker (see table 4.3). Adjusting for differences in population size, in 1980 black men's total hourly earnings were only 52 percent of

Figure 4.5   White Wage Advantage of Men Ages Twenty to Thirty-Four, 1980 to 2008

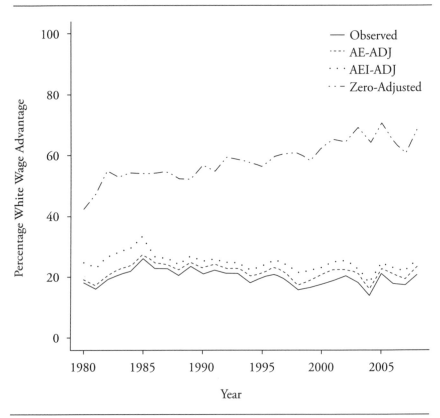

Source: Author's calculations of data from Pettit, Sykes, and Western (2009).
Notes: The age-education adjustment (AE-ADJ) assumes that inmates earn comparable wages to similarly skilled men observed in the labor force. The age-education-incarceration adjustment (AEI-ADJ) assumes that inmates experience a wage penalty in proportion to their wages relative to similarly skilled men prior to incarceration. Zero-ADJ includes the jobless earning zero wages. See the methodological appendix for more details.

white men's total hourly earnings (shown in the top line in figure 4.5 labeled "Zero-Adjusted"). Not only did black men earn less per hour worked, but fewer black men were working in paid employment. By 2008, black earnings had fallen to 38 percent of white men's earnings on a per capita basis. While black men in the labor force were faring as well as they had in 1980 compared to whites, relatively fewer black men were working.

Table 4.3   Percentage of White Men's Wages Earned by Blacks, Including the Jobless, 1980 to 2008

	1980	1990	2000	2008
Eighteen to sixty-four	52.1%	39.2%	35.0%	27.9%
Twenty to thirty-four	57.6	42.9	37.3	30.9
Twenty to thirty-four with less than a high school degree	57.1	41.9	35.8	29.6

Source: Author's calculations. See the methodological appendix for more details.

Increasing black unemployment—including that resulting from incarceration—combined with declining earnings among workers has halved the relative economic position of young black men. In 1980 young black men earned almost 58 percent of white men's hourly wages. Because of steep increases in joblessness due to incarceration and other factors, by 2008 blacks earned on average 30 cents on every white-earned dollar. Claims of improvements in the economic standing of black men, and of young black men in particular, are often supported by analysis of conventional data sources that exclude the incarcerated. Unfortunately, the men who are incarcerated have among the poorest economic fortunes of any social group, and their exclusion leads to growing sample selection bias. Including them in accounts of the well-being of the population contributes to a much less optimistic story of the relative economic standing of blacks in America through the first decade of the twenty-first century.

CONCLUSION

National statistics like the high school dropout rate, employment rates, and the black-white wage gap cannot be taken at face value. Education, employment, and wage differentials are embedded in broader patterns of racially differentiated social exclusion, such as incarceration. Estimates of the educational attainment and economic capacities of the population and of racial inequality are fundamentally obscured by the sample selection effects induced by decades of penal expansion and race and class inequality in incarceration rates.

Among black men, including inmates in national estimates implies a nationwide high school dropout rate more than 40 percent higher than suggested by conventional estimates that use the Current Population Survey.

Similar bias is found for conventional estimates of employment and wages. In 2008 nearly one in five young black men did not finish high school, black male dropouts were more likely to be in prison than to be employed, and relative wages among young black men had seen little improvement over the previous twenty years.

Illusions of black educational and economic progress, however, have been sustained by reliance on data sources that categorically exclude prison and jail inmates from estimates of the educational attainment and economic activity of the population. Just as Darity (1980) documented how the exclusion of the unemployed from calculations of wages overestimated the economic progress of blacks and obscured the extent of racial inequality in the labor market, the exclusion of inmates from conventional data sources conceals the magnitude of racial inequality in educational and economic outcomes.

These results call into question the reliance on sample surveys of households to make generalizations about the American population. Recent research has suggested that the Current Population Survey is the gold standard for estimating the educational attainment of the population (Goldin and Katz 2008). Trends in educational attainment generated by the Current Population Survey are commonly used by researchers and policymakers to make claims about the state of education in the United States and to allocate public resources toward educational programs and objectives. However, the Current Population Survey's reliance on a household sampling frame does limit its generalizability in an era of mass incarceration.

These results also call into question whether and to what extent the current educational system offers a path to social mobility for disadvantaged groups. Black men have experienced no improvement in high school completion rates since the early 1990s, and significant racial inequality in educational attainment among men persists even five decades after Brown v. Board of Education. Such findings call into question the assumed egalitarian effects of the educational system.

The consequences of continued racial inequality in educational attainment are noteworthy given the association between education and incarceration. The education system contributes to particularly high dropout rates for black men, who then face a high risk of incarceration. As a result, incarceration has become a normative life course event for low-skill black men. Ironically, the link between the education and penal systems obscures the inequality-reproducing effects of the education system. The groups most poorly served by the education system have the lowest levels of educational attainment and are the most likely to be incarcerated and excluded from the probability-based samples of households commonly used to estimate educational attainment.

The criminal justice system rivals deindustrialization and segregation in its effects on the educational and economic opportunities of black men. The evidence presented in this chapter calls into question whether and to what extent the penal system constitutes a system of social exclusion so profound that it compares to slavery and Jim Crow (Wacquant 2000, 2001; Alexander 2010). It certainly must be considered in the construction of accounts of educational and economic inequalities and the factors thought to produce them. As a repository for America's high school dropouts, the penal system concentrates and conceals the most deeply disadvantaged from social science research, social policymakers, and the public to create illusions of progress.

CHAPTER 5

Democracy in the Age of Mass Incarceration

> And I pledge you that we will not delay, or we will not hesitate, or we will not turn aside until Americans of every race and color and origin in this country have the same right as all others to share in the process of democracy.
>
> —Lyndon B. Johnson, statement on signing the Voting Rights Act, August 6, 1965

The concealing effects of incarceration on racial inequality are not limited to educational and economic outcomes. One of the most studied phenomena of contemporary American politics is the decline in voter turnout, which was particularly acute from 1960 to 1988. Turnout edged up in 1992, only to plummet again in 1996. Although there was a general resurgence in voter turnout in the 2000s, overall turnout rates remain well below their 1960 peak.

In contrast to the overall decline in voter turnout from 1960 through the late 1990s, turnout rates among African Americans rose through the 1960s and have generally held steady since the mid-1970s. At least a portion of the early increase in African American turnout was attributed to the Voting Rights Act of 1965, though voter turnout among blacks had been on the rise since at least 1948 (Filer, Kenny, and Morton 1991; Lawson 1976, 1985). After a steep upturn in voter turnout among blacks through the 2000s, turnout among African Americans in 2008, an election that featured Barack Obama, rivaled that among whites for the first time since the Current Popu-

Figure 5.1 Trends in Voter Turnout Rates for Men Ages Twenty to Thirty-Four, 1980 to 2008

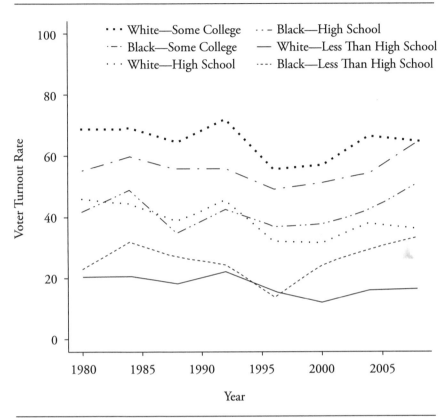

Source: Author's calculations of data from Rosenfeld et al. (2010).

lation Survey began collecting data on voter turnout. The 2008 election posted the highest rates of black turnout on record.

The data from the Current Population Survey shown in figure 5.1 clearly demonstrate that voter turnout for young black men surpassed that of young white men in 2008. The figure traces the fraction of the population, within race and education groups, that reported voting in the presidential elections. The solid black line at the bottom of the figure, for example, shows voter turnout rates among white men who had not completed high school. Consistent with data reported in table 5.2 the figure shows that the voter turnout rate in this group fluctuated from 20.4 percent in 1980 to 16.5 percent in 2008.

The figure shows that voter turnout rates for young black men, across all education groups, increased between 1996 and 2008. Even groups at the highest risk of incarceration, including young, low-skill, black men, saw an upsurge in voter turnout rates in 2008. Analysts from the Pew Research Center (2009, ii) noted that, for the first time, "the voter turnout rate among young, black eligible voters was higher than that of any other racial and ethnic group in 2008." Alternately attributed to candidate Barack Obama's race, charisma, or political organization (see, for example, Philpot, Shaw, and McGowen 2009), high turnout among young and minority voters was noted as a key factor in Obama's electoral victory.

At the same time that evidence indicates a resurgence of voting among historically disenfranchised groups, social scientists argue that the felon disenfranchisement associated with criminal justice expansion has altered the contours of American democracy (Manza and Uggen 2006). High rates of incarceration coupled with voting restrictions tied to felony convictions are hypothesized to have disenfranchised a growing number of minority voters, presumably with an impact on numerous electoral outcomes, most notably Bush versus Gore in 2000 (Manza and Uggen 2006). A felony conviction carries short- and possibly long-term restrictions on voting in forty-eight states. Table 5.1 lists the voting restrictions, by state, associated with felony convictions.

How can we reconcile claims of increased voter turnout in the most recent election with growing levels of disenfranchisement among those purported to have turned out in record numbers? High rates of voter turnout among young black men and claims of record turnout among African Americans in the 2008 election that featured Barack Obama are at least partially an artifact of growing incarceration. Although including ineligible voters such as noncitizens and those with a felony conviction in counts of voter turnout deflates overall estimates of voter turnout (McDonald and Popkin 2001), excluding institutionalized persons from the Current Population Survey inflates voter turnout in groups with high incarceration rates by removing large segments of the population from estimates of voter turnout.

New research by Traci Burch (2010) suggests that convicted felons are unlikely voters even prior to incarceration. Data from Florida show that 9.4 percent of incarcerated felons voted prior to incarceration. Comparable rates were 16.7 percent in Georgia, 11.7 percent in Missouri, and 17.3 percent in North Carolina (Burch 2010). Burch's research shows that even among those

Table 5.1   Disenfranchisement Categories under State Law, 2010

State	Prison	Probation	Parole	All	Post-Sentence
Alabama	X	X	X		X (certain offenses)
Arizona	X	X	X		
Arkansas	X	X	X		X (second felony)
California	X	X	X		
Colorado	X		X		
Connecticut	X		X		
Delaware	X	X	X		X (certain offenses five years)
District of Columbia	X				
Florida	X	X	X		X (certain offenses)
Georgia	X	X	X		
Hawaii	X				
Idaho	X	X	X		
Illinois	X				
Indiana	X				
Iowa	X	X	X		
Kansas	X	X	X		
Kentucky	X	X	X	X	
Louisiana	X	X	X		
Maine					
Maryland	X	X	X		
Massachusetts	X				
Michigan	X				
Minnesota	X	X	X		
Mississippi	X	X	X		X (certain offenses)
Missouri	X	X	X		
Montana	X				
Nebraska	X	X	X		X (two years)
Nevada	X	X	X		X (except first-time nonviolent)
New Hampshire	X				
New Jersey	X	X	X		
New Mexico	X	X	X		
New York	X		X		

(*Table continues on p. 74.*)

Table 5.1   *(continued)*

State	Prison	Probation	Parole	All	Post-Sentence
North Carolina	X	X	X		
North Dakota	X				
Ohio	X				
Oklahoma	X	X	X		
Oregon	X				
Pennsylvania	X				
Rhode Island	X				
South Carolina	X	X	X		
South Dakota	X		X		
Tennessee	X	X	X		X (certain offenses)
Texas	X	X	X		
Utah	X				
Vermont					
Virginia	X	X	X	X	
Washington	X	X	X		
West Virginia	X	X	X		
Wisconsin	X	X	X		
Wyoming	X	X	X		X (certain offenses five years)
United States Total	49	30	35	2	9

Source: Author's compilation of data from The Sentencing Project (2010).

registered to vote, a very low proportion of felons exercise the option. Thus, removing current inmates from sample surveys of the population generates a pool of "eligible voters" more likely to turn out than the general population.

As the penal population has grown, it has siphoned more and more unregistered and unlikely voters from the samples used to construct estimates of the voter turnout rate, including the Current Population Survey and the National Election Survey (NES). As a consequence, recent increases in voter turnout and especially high rates of voter turnout in high-incarceration subgroups are at least partially the result of continued reliance on the household-based probability sampling methods employed by the Current Population Survey and the National Election Survey. Excluding currently incarcerated inmates who are unable to vote in forty-eight states from surveys like the Current Population Survey inflates turnout rates in precisely those groups that are most likely to be disenfranchised by mass incarceration.

VOTING RIGHTS AND MASS INCARCERATION

A majority of African American men voted in all but two southern states in the 1880 presidential election (Kousser 1975, cited in Filer et al. 1991). One hundred years later, in 1980, fewer than half (49.7 percent) of black men voted in the presidential election. It took four more years for a majority of black men to cast a ballot in a presidential election. Data from surveys of the non-institutionalized population show that majorities of black men have voted in all of the presidential elections since then—except in 1996, when overall turnout rates plummeted.

After Reconstruction, many states instituted a number of voting restrictions that reduced the electoral participation of African Americans. Poll taxes, literacy tests, and separate ballot boxes were common in much of the South until the Voting Rights Acts of 1965 and 1970. Poll taxes were common in the South until the Voting Rights Act of 1965, and literacy tests were in effect in as many as twenty states until they were outlawed by the Voting Rights Act of 1970. Alaska, California, Connecticut, Delaware, Hawaii, Louisiana, Maine, Massachusetts, New Hampshire, North Carolina, South Carolina, Virginia, Washington, and Wyoming all had voter literacy tests in place through the presidential contest of 1968 (Filer et al. 1991).

Poll taxes and literacy tests disproportionately affected the eligibility of African American voters. Because blacks faced higher risks of poverty and lower levels of educational attainment and literacy than native-born whites, they bore the brunt of voting restrictions. Evidence suggests that black political involvement was relatively high immediately after Reconstruction but languished during the early twentieth century (Tushnet 1987). Voting restrictions, combined with Jim Crow–era segregation, effectively disenfranchised several generations of African Americans (Tushnet 1987).

Opposition to the disenfranchisement of black voters percolated throughout the 1900s. The NAACP championed challenges to de jure segregation as early as 1929 (Ashenfelter, Collins, and Yoon 2006; Tushnet 1987). Widespread political mobilization of African Americans began in earnest after World War II (see, for example, Andrews 1997). Voter turnout among African Americans was 37 percent nationwide when Truman unexpectedly beat Dewey in 1948 (American National Election Studies 2005). Active political organization in the 1950s and 1960s was associated with a dramatic increase in voter turnout among blacks even before the Voting Rights Acts of 1965 and 1970. In the 1960 presidential contest between Richard Nixon and John F. Kennedy, 53 percent of blacks voted, representing a 43 percent increase over 1948 levels. Over the next eight years, voter turnout among African Americans would rise another 23 percent. Nearly two-thirds (65 percent) of eligible black voters cast ballots in the first presidential election after the 1965 Voting Rights Act (American National Election Studies 2005).

Scholars and pundits have suggested that advocacy groups and social movement organizations contributed to the dramatic growth in voter turnout rates among blacks and the high turnout rates even among those with low levels of education (see, for example, Philpot et al. 2009; Andrews 1997). African American churches and political organizations in particular played a unique role in bridging socioeconomic divides by incorporating non-elite African Americans into the political sphere (Liu, Austin, and Orey 2009; Tate 1991). Targeted black outreach has been shown to influence black turnout (Gerber and Green 2000; Green, Gerber, and Nickerson 2003), and voter mobilization through organizations in the African American community is thought to reduce turnout gaps between blacks and whites and between more-advantaged and less-advantaged blacks.

There is empirical evidence consistent with the argument that voter turnout among blacks is influenced less by education and socioeconomic status than it is among whites. This lends credence to explanations that emphasize the central importance of institutions for getting out the black vote. Highly educated whites are significantly more likely to vote than less-educated whites. Although there is an education gap in voter turnout between more- and less-educated blacks, it is far less dramatic than that found among whites. Research shows that indicators like education and income have smaller effects on the probability of political participation for blacks compared to whites (Liu et al. 2009; Philpot et al. 2009; see also Leighley and Vedlitz 1999).

Consistent with long-standing explanations for voter participation among blacks, churches and political organizations were thought to be particularly effective in getting out the black vote in the 2008 presidential election that featured Barack Obama. Tasha Philpot and her colleagues (2009, 997) argue that "higher levels of political interest, efficacy, and shared racial identity among Black voters were not necessarily the main story behind the increase in Black turnout" in 2008. Instead, party contacting efforts drove increases in black turnout. Obama's outreach effort included targeting black churches as well as going door to door in an attempt to mobilize black voters (Philpot et al. 2009).

Mass incarceration suggests the importance of a different kind of institution—namely, prisons and jails—for understanding political participation among black men. Mass incarceration has two effects. First, it narrows the electorate by reducing the number of eligible voters through various felon disenfranchisement laws. Second, it contributes to the growing sample selection bias associated with the exclusion of inmates from the household-based sample surveys of the population used to generate accounts of the voting-eligible population. Just as churches and political organizations influence voter turnout, so does mass incarceration. Incarceration, however, not only determines who is eligible to vote but also who is counted in voting statistics.

INCORPORATING INCARCERATION IN VOTER TURNOUT

To what extent do comparatively high turnout rates and low levels of political inequality among blacks result from excluding prison and jail inmates from conventional surveys of voting behavior? Table 5.2 shows estimates of voter turnout using just Current Population Survey data and adjusted estimates that include the prison and jail population. In 1980, adding the prison and jail populations to CPS samples results in essentially unchanged turnout rates among young white men. The adjustment to turnout rates for young blacks was more substantial, averaging 5.1 percent. Among the subgroup with the highest incarceration rate—young, low-skill, black men—turnout rates are overstated by just above 10 percent.

For 2008, however, estimates of voter turnout that include inmates generate sizable adjustments in turnout rates among young, low-skill, white men and contradict claims of a recent uptick in voter turnout among young black men. Adjusting for mass incarceration indicates that a minority of young black men voted in 2008 (48.6 percent). Contrary to numerous reports that young blacks outvoted whites in the 2008 election, young white men outvoted blacks by 3.4 percentage points in 2008. It is the case that black men with low levels of education voted at greater rates than similarly educated

Table 5.2   Adjusted and Unadjusted Voter Turnout Estimates for Men Ages Twenty to Thirty-Four, by Education, 1980 to 2008

	Unadjusted	Adjusted	Percentage Difference
1980			
White, college	68.6%	68.5%	0.1%
White, high school	45.8	45.5	0.7
White, less than high school	20.4	20.1	1.5
White, all	55.2	54.9	0.5
Black, college	55.3	54.4	1.7
Black, high school	41.5	39.5	5.1
Black, less than high school	22.8	20.7	10.1
Black, all	42.0	40.0	5.1
2008			
White, college	64.9	64.6	0.5
White, high school	36.4	35.7	2.0
White, less than high school	16.5	14.4	14.6
White, all	53.0	52.1	1.7
Black, college	64.3	63.0	2.1
Black, high school	50.8	46.1	10.2
Black, less than high school	33.5	20.4	64.2
Black, all	55.0	48.6	13.2

Source: Author's calculations using data from the March Current Population Survey (U.S. Census Bureau, various years) and data from the Bureau of Justice Statistics Surveys of Inmates (U.S. Dept. of Justice, BJS, various years–a, various years–b, various years–c). See the methodological appendix for more details.

whites in 2008. The explanation, however, lies not in the increased exercise of the franchise among blacks. Instead, continued declines in voter turnout among poorly educated whites have led to record low turnout in that group.

Data from 2008 provide clear evidence that the exclusion of prison and jail inmates from voting statistics results in severely inflated turnout rates for sociodemographic groups with high incarceration rates. Among whites age eighteen to sixty-four, high school dropouts turned out to vote at rates 8 percent lower than what is typically reported for the 2008 election. The incarceration adjustment lowers the turnout rate among black dropouts of working age (eighteen to sixty-four) in 2008 by over one-third (36 percent).

Among young men age twenty to thirty-four, including inmates in voter turnout estimates suggests that conventional surveys overstated the 2008 turnout rate among whites by 1.8 percent and among blacks by 11.5 percent. The effects of incarceration among young male dropouts is dramatic: the voter turnout rate in the 2008 election is overstated by close to 15 percent among whites and nearly two-thirds (64.2 percent) among young, black, male dropouts.

Steep increases in incarceration since 1980 have profoundly affected trends in the voter turnout rate among disadvantaged men. Although conventional wisdom suggests that the turnout rate among low-skill black men increased by 50 percent from 1980 to 2008, the increase was entirely driven by the selective removal of nonvoters from household-based surveys. In fact, adjusting for sample selectivity due to incarceration indicates that turnout rates among young black men were only 2.5 percentage points higher in 2008 than in 1984 (48.6 percent to 46.1 percent). And among young black high school dropouts, turnout rates declined by a small margin from 1980 to 2008, even though unadjusted data suggest that turnout grew dramatically.

Evidence supports the conventional wisdom and the commonly used data, which find a narrowing of the race gap in the voter turnout rate among young men. The race gap in voting peaked in 1992, and young black men are now almost as likely to vote as are young white men. However, the narrowing of the race gap in the voter turnout rate is not as dramatic as conventional data sources imply, and young black men do not vote as commonly as young white men (see figure 5.2). Much of the reported narrowing of the race gap in the voter turnout rate is attributable to the exclusionary effects of mass incarceration. The rest results from declines in the turnout rate among whites and not from widespread increases in the democratic participation of young black men.

CONCLUSION

High rates of incarceration disenfranchise large segments of the American electorate. Jeff Manza and Christopher Uggen (2006) estimate that 16 million Americans were disenfranchised owing to felony convictions in the mid-2000s. Like poll taxes, literacy tests, and separate ballot boxes, mass incarcera-

Figure 5.2   Revised Trends in Voter Turnout Rates of Men Ages
              Twenty to Thirty-Four, by Education, 1980 to 2008

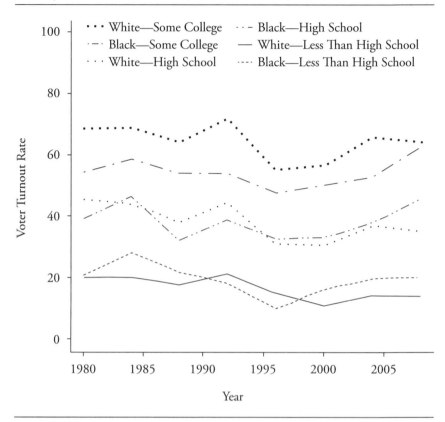

Source: Author's calculations of data from Rosenfeld et al. (2010).

tion disproportionately disenfranchises blacks. Recent data suggest that 13
percent of black men are excluded from the democratic franchise because of
their involvement in the criminal justice system (Sentencing Project 2010).

The full extent of the disenfranchisement exacted by mass incarceration is
obscured by estimates of the voter turnout rate that are generated from surveys of the household-based population. Conventional data sources show a
resurgence in voting through the 2000s, and 2008 witnessed the highest
turnout rates among young blacks ever recorded. Explanations for the democratic engagement of black youth emphasize that institutions like black
churches and the Democratic Party, along with a charismatic black candidate,
brought out the vote.

The number of votes cast in the 2008 election certainly broke records, but the voter turnout rate did not. There is little question about the number of people who voted, but there is quite a lot of doubt about what fraction of the population voted. The controversy lies in who to include in turnout statistics. Political scientists have long been aware that the data used to estimate voter turnout rates are subject to problems associated with estimating the "ineligible" population (McDonald and Popkin 2001).

If turnout is to be used as a measure of the democratic participation of a particular group, we would do well to consider what fraction of a social or demographic group exercised the franchise. This may be thought of as a vote-to-population ratio. As such, it tells us little about the presence of potential voters—information that may be relevant to candidates, party advocates, or get-out-the-vote activists—but something very important about the political participation of particular social and demographic groups.

The exclusion of currently incarcerated individuals from estimates of voter turnout inflates measures of the turnout rate among sociodemographic groups with high incarceration rates. Therefore, excluding inmates from the Current Population Survey creates the illusion of growing democratic engagement among the segment of the population that is increasingly disenfranchised, young black men. In fact, a declining fraction of young black men are eligible to vote, owing to the exclusionary effects of mass incarceration. Whether or for whom they would vote if they could is a thorny question, and one on which there is significant debate (Miles 2004; Manza and Uggen 2006; Burch 2010).

Including inmates in estimates of voter turnout helps to reconcile the seemingly inconsistent evidence of increases in disenfranchisement associated with mass incarceration with the claims of record turnout among young black men in the election of Barack Obama. The perception of the growing political involvement of young black men is simply an illusion, an artifact of survey methods that predate penal expansion. Felons—and ex-felons in some states—are excluded not only from the franchise but also from many official accounts of the population, including those that gauge voter turnout. Voter turnout statistics are now generated on the basis of the experiences of an increasingly select and advantaged population relative to those excluded. Incorporating inmates into their construction betrays the illusion of growing political involvement among young black men and illuminates the extent of their political disenfranchisement.

The expansion of the carceral state systematically undermines the political power of the constituency most directly affected by it. The level of democratic engagement among young blacks is not, as some have argued, at historic highs (Pew Research Center 2009). On the contrary, whole segments of the black population are excluded from the political process. Less than half of young black men cast a ballot in the election that featured the man who would become America's first black president. And among black high school dropouts, only one in five voted in the 2008 election—exactly the same fraction that voted in the 1980 election, in which Ronald Reagan trounced Jimmy Carter.

As the criminal justice system has grown, the economic and political fortunes of the most disadvantaged segments of the American population have stagnated or declined. Not only is this true for the men and women in prison and jail, but as the next chapter will show in detail, children, families, and communities are also subject to the destabilizing effects of mass incarceration. Mass incarceration undermines economic capacity and civic participation in America's most disadvantaged communities. Once again, our national data systems help keep the extent of that disadvantage hidden from public view.

CHAPTER 6

Other Casualties of Mass Incarceration

The question is not whether we can afford to invest in every child; it is whether we can afford not to.
—Marian Wright Edelman, *The Measure of Our Success* (1992)

America's more than three-decade-long war on crime has generated the largest prison system in the world. And just as some crimes involve innocent victims, there are numerous casualties of penal expansion. The growth of the prison system represents a critical institutional intervention in the lives of American children, families, and the most disadvantaged communities. Children are perhaps the most unwitting victims. A growing share of American children now face the prospect of having a parent incarcerated at some point during their childhood. Incapacitation by the criminal justice system not only shapes the lives of adult inmates but has potentially long-term effects on their children.

The number of children in the United States with a parent incarcerated has increased fivefold since 1980. Figure 6.1 shows that approximately 500,000 children under age eighteen had a parent in prison or jail on any given day in 1980. By 2008, the number of minors with a parent in prison or jail had eclipsed 2.6 million. Owing to racial disproportionality in incarceration, by 2008 there were more black children with a parent in prison or jail than children of any race or ethnicity with an incarcerated parent in 1980. The vast majority of parents in prison are guilty of nonviolent property and drug offenses. In 2008 over 1.7 million children had a parent who was incarcerated for a nonviolent offense.

Figure 6.1   Number of Children with a Parent in Prison or Jail, by Race, 1980 to 2008

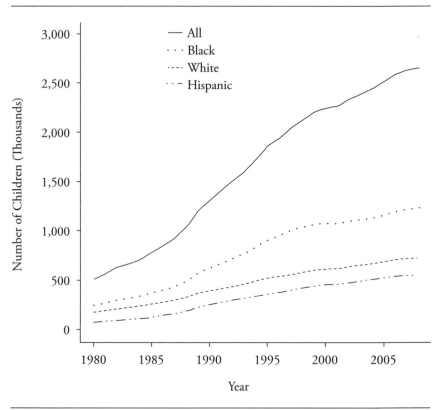

Source: Author's calculations of data from Pettit, Sykes, and Western (2009).

Regardless of the crime committed, parental incarceration is likely to contribute to instability in family life. Over half of all prisoners have children under the age of eighteen, and about 45 percent of those parents were living with their children at the time they were sent to prison. In addition to the forced separation of incarceration, the postrelease effects on economic opportunities leave formerly incarcerated parents less equipped to provide financially for their children. Incarceration is known to depress marriage and cohabitation among unwed parents (Wilson 1987; Edin, Nelson, and Paranal 2004; Western, Lopoo, and McLanahan 2004; Lopoo and Western 2005). New research also shows that the children of incarcerated parents, particularly boys, are at greater risk of developmental delays and behavioral problems (Wildeman 2010; Geller et al. 2011; Geller et al., forthcoming).

America's most disadvantaged communities have been acutely affected by mass incarceration. The concentration of incarceration among particular social and demographic groups combines with high rates of residential segregation by race and class to keep America's prison and jail population coming from and returning to relatively few areas. According to Rose Heyer and Peter Wagner (2004), for example, 60 percent of Illinois prisoners are from Cook County (Chicago). James Lynch and William Sabol (2001) estimate that in 1996 fully two-thirds of state prison releases were to what they call "core counties": a county that contains the central city of a metropolitan area. And research by Jeffrey Morenoff and David Harding (2011) in Michigan finds that 12 percent of Census tracts receive 50 percent of parolees from Michigan state prisons and 2 percent of tracts receive 25 percent. A disproportionate number of released inmates from Michigan state prisons head to Wayne County and its seat, Detroit (Morenoff et al. 2009).

Prison and jail inmates are also geographically concentrated while incapacitated, though typically not in the same communities where they lived before being incarcerated and to which they are likely to return. According to data from the 2000 Census, Ward 2 in Anamosa, Iowa, has twenty-two inmates for every non-institutionalized resident (*New York Times* 2008). In twenty-one counties in the United States, at least one-fifth of the population lives in correctional institutions (Heyer and Wagner 2004). Nearly all (99 percent) Illinois inmates who hail from Cook County serve their sentences in other counties (Heyer and Wagner 2004). The geographic concentration of inmates in communities distant from where they lived before incapacitation is associated with growing numbers of African Americans in rural areas living in state and federal prisons.

Like the effects of incarceration on the educational, economic, and political outcomes of inmates, the full extent of the prison system's influence on children, families, and communities is largely obscured by conventional surveys that categorically ignore and systematically undercount inmates and former inmates. Government policies and practices have long affected portraits of the American family and community life. Nearly 150 years after Reconstruction, scholars still debate the effects of slavery on accounts of the black family (see, for example, Gutman 1976; Franklin 1997; Dunaway 2003; Mc-

Daniel 1995). Some argue that slavery led to a distinctive pattern of family life among African Americans characterized by high rates of single parenthood, father absence, and intergenerational families (see, for example, Dunaway 2003; McDaniel 1995). Others contend that the family lives of black and white children were remarkably similar even on plantations: black children living on large southern plantations were as likely to live in two-parent families as were white children (Gutman 1976).

Much of the debate over black family life stems from questions over how to reconstruct the lives of slaves and their families. As mentioned in chapter 2, at least until the Census of 1850, few detailed data were systematically collected on the experiences of black Americans. The names of African Americans were not systematically recorded on Census forms until 1850, and even then, supplemental schedules for slaves included only age, gender, and information about race (U.S. Census Bureau 2008a). Historians have combed through archival material in their attempts to discern patterns of black family life in relation to geography, economic activity, and slave-holding before and after Reconstruction, but information about the family life of black Americans prior to Reconstruction has remained remarkably sparse.

Contemporary data systems are based on the assumption that people live in settled households, and they do not account for the transience and institutionalization common in some sociodemographic groups. The living arrangements of inmates before, during, and after incapacitation contribute to their absence from many data sources, including public records. The prison system removes individuals from the general population and confines them for a specified period of time during which they are not included in federal survey efforts focused on the household population. The incarceration-associated elision of some aspects of black family life from federal data collection efforts has coincided with claims of decreased federal involvement in the lives of Americans (Western 2006).

The exclusion of inmates from conventional data sources inhibits scholars and policymakers from fully accounting for the effects of incarceration on children. No single survey collects data that make it easy to determine how many or what fraction of children have a parent in prison. Most federally sponsored surveys do not ask about the incarceration histories of respondents or family members. The federal government does not systematically collect data on where prison inmates hail from or where they plan to live after release from prison or jail. Only by careful fieldwork or piecing together information from surveys of the institutionalized population with information from other sources can we begin to understand the extent of the collateral damage from the extraordinary growth of the penal system.

INCARCERATION AND FAMILY LIFE

The impact of parental incarceration on children and families may be the least understood, yet most consequential, implication of mass incarceration (Hagan and Dinovitzer 1999). Estimates suggest that 3.6 percent of minor children of any race or ethnicity had a parent in prison or jail in 2008 (Pettit et al. 2009). One in fifty-seven white children (1.8 percent) compared to one in nine African American children (11.4 percent) had a mother or father incarcerated (Pettit et al. 2009). Data from the National Survey of Adolescent Health (Adhealth) indicate that as many as 12 percent of recent cohorts of children have had a biological father in prison or jail at some point in their childhood (Foster and Hagan 2007). Christopher Wildeman's (2009) careful analysis of the risk of parental imprisonment finds that one-quarter of recent cohorts of black children can expect to have a parent imprisoned during their childhood.

Table 6.1 compares the risk of parental imprisonment by age seventeen for children born prior to penal expansion and for those born during its height. In 1980 fewer than half a percent of white children and fewer than 3 percent of black children experienced parental imprisonment by age seventeen. By 2009, those numbers had increased dramatically. Consistent with estimates produced by Wildeman (2009), table 6.1 shows that approximately 4 percent of white children and one-quarter of black children had a parent in prison at some point in their childhood. The numbers are staggering for children with poorly educated parents. Among recent cohorts of children of high school dropouts, 14.5 percent of white children and 62 percent of black children had a parent who went to prison before they reached age seventeen.

The quantitative evidence on the consequences of incarceration for children and families is still nascent, yet many qualitative studies have effectively demonstrated how incarceration affects the family lives and the children of those involved in the criminal justice system. By spending extended periods of time with inmates, former inmates, and their families and conducting intensive interviews, researchers have gathered an impressive body of evidence documenting the effects of incarceration on families and children, carefully considering the pathways through which incarceration influences family life. Their findings have drawn attention to the impact on parenting and partner-

Table 6.1   Cumulative Risk of Parental Imprisonment by Age Seventeen, by Education, 1980 to 2009

	1980		2009	
	Non-Hispanic White	Non-Hispanic Black	Non-Hispanic White	Non-Hispanic Black
Less than high school	1.3%	5.5%	14.5%	62.1%
High school/GED	0.5	2.2	3.7	16.1
Some college	0.1	1.2	1.4	9.9
All	0.4	2.9	4.0	24.2

Source: Author's calculations. See the methodological appendix for more details.
Note: The 1980 cohort was born between 1960 and 1964; the 2009 cohort was born between 1989 and 1993.

ing of removing individuals from their families and the associated economic hardship and social stigma.

John Hagan and Ronit Dinovitzer (1999) argue that the loss of a father to incarceration changes the family's status to that of a single-parent family, ushering in effects similar to those brought on by the death of a parent or divorce, such as financial instability and emotional and psychological effects on the children and partner. These issues are examined in Donald Braman's book *Doing Time on the Outside* (2004), in which he provides an account of the impact of mass incarceration on families and communities in Washington, D.C. Braman demonstrates that incarceration levies financial costs that extend well beyond the individual incarcerated, and that the psychological and social stigma of having a family member in prison or jail undermines the social fabric of urban communities.

In *Doing Time Together* (2008), Megan Comfort details the experiences of women attempting to maintain relationships with men at San Quentin State Prison. Although the women she studied were free to leave San Quentin after their visits, the prison—and the men they loved who lived there—shaped their experiences and opportunities, burdening them financially and psychologically. Using the Fragile Families and Child Well-being Study, Amanda Geller and her colleagues (2009) confirm, with quantitative data, the extent to which incarceration separates fathers from the labor force, making them unable to contribute financially to the needs of their partners and children.

Although the financial effects of paternal incarceration may be greatest during periods of incapacitation, financial hardship affects previously incarcerated inmates and their families long after release (Comfort 2008). In her book *My Baby's Father* (2002), Maureen Waller demonstrates how men's poor economic opportunities—shaped by previous contact with the criminal justice system—structure their involvement in their children's lives. Fathers' involvement in their children's lives may be curtailed, she argues, by their limited employment prospects and inability to contribute to the financial well-being of their children. Geller and her colleagues (forthcoming) also demonstrate that fathers' ability to contribute to the financial well-being of the family is curtailed even after release from prison or jail.

Evidence suggests that fathers who have been incarcerated are much less likely to be cohabiting or married a year after their babies' birth (Western et al. 2004). Incarceration can also trigger a higher risk of divorce or separation. Drawing on data from the National Longitudinal Survey of Youth 1979 (NLSY-79), Leonard Lopoo and Bruce Western (2005) find that the likelihood that a marriage will fail in the year a man is incarcerated is over three times higher than that for a man who is not incarcerated (13 percent to 4 percent). Incarceration is thought to affect cohabitation and marriage directly through its incapacitative effect and indirectly through its implications for economic opportunities and social stigma (see, for example, Edin and Kefalas 2005).

The effects of incarceration on the well-being of children are only beginning to be understood. Children of incarcerated fathers are more likely to receive public assistance and more likely to experience material hardship, disruptive residential mobility, and greater risk for developmental outcomes such as aggressive behavior (Geller et al., forthcoming). Children of incarcerated parents are commonly pushed into kinship care or formal foster care (Freudenberg 2001). Finding that families of inmates were at risk for financial and mental health instability even prior to incarceration, Joyce Arditti, Jennifer Lambert-Shute, and Karen Joest (2003) emphasize that incarceration elevates the risks of hardship among the already vulnerable.

Comfort (2008) finds that seeing a father arrested, visiting him in prison, and dealing with parental absence traumatizes children. Children of incarcerated fathers, Comfort argues, witness parental disempowerment and must contend with the emotional and psychological effects of the abrupt removal of a parent as well as the quasi-imprisonment associated with the many rules and procedures involved in visiting a parent in correctional facilities. Anne Nurse (2004) demonstrates that incarcerated fathers' involvement in their children's lives is shaped by the children's mother and that hostility between young parents can have negative implications for children. Christopher Wildeman (2010) demonstrates that recent and prior paternal incarceration is associated with significantly higher levels of physically aggressive behaviors in boys at age five. In a review of existing research, Sara Wakefield and Wildeman (2011) find that children who have had a parent incarcerated experience increases in mental health and behavioral problems as well as increases in the level of their physical aggression.

Despite important insights gleaned from existing research, the social scientific and policy communities have been slow to respond to the shifts in family life associated with mass incarceration and to collect nationally representative data designed to investigate the implications of incarceration for families and children. Few national surveys collect information about reasons for father absence, and no national statistics are produced on the number of children living in single-parent families because of parental incarceration. Although data from the National Study of Adolescent Health (Adhealth) and the Fragile Families Study have advanced our understanding of the effects of incarceration for families with young children, there is still much we do not know and cannot understand from existing large-scale data sources.

THE GEOGRAPHY OF INCARCERATION

The effects of mass incarceration are most acutely felt in America's disadvantaged communities (see, for example, Clear 2007). Data from the Census can be used to construct the geographic distribution of inmates while they are incarcerated, but researchers have generally had to rely on qualitative and ethnographic research to frame our understanding of the impact of incarceration on the social fabric of communities with high levels of incarceration. Census data confirm that the exclusionary effects of incapacitation profoundly influence contemporary statistics on the geographic distribution of the population, and the qualitative and ethnographic research illustrates that the criminal justice system and incarceration do indeed have an impact on social engagement and community life.

Through the early 1900s, African Americans in the United States were disproportionately concentrated in the rural South. During World War I, large numbers of southern blacks moved to northern cities in search of economic opportunities and to escape the racial tensions of the Jim Crow South. One and a half million African Americans moved from the South primarily to northern cities between 1910 and 1940, and another four million moved out of the South between 1940 and 1970 (Hahn 2003; Lemann 1991). By 1970, only one in five blacks lived in rural areas. Outside of the South, 97 percent of blacks lived in urban areas (Cahill 1974).

Penal system growth reverses a century-long trend of blacks moving from rural areas into more urban ones. Inmates are often relocated to serve prison sentences outside of their own primarily urban communities into disproportionately rural areas. Mass incarceration therefore results in the movement of inmates—disproportionately male, low-skill, and black—into rural areas. Recent evidence suggests that parolees return to urban communities after their release from prison (Morenoff and Harding 2011). However, quantitative data on the effects of incarceration on residential mobility, instability, and homelessness are sparse, thereby limiting our understanding of the full range of impacts wielded by mass incarceration.

Students of the U.S. Census have recognized small but growing communities of color in suburban and rural locations across the country. Some of these population shifts do not reflect voluntary migration but instead result from the growth of the prison system. A growing fraction of communities of color in rural and suburban locations represent the relocation of disproportionately poor and black urban residents into suburban and rural prisons, but if attention is limited to those living in households, that observation is easily overlooked.

Data gathered from the non-institutionalized population do not reflect the new geography associated with mass incarceration. Table 6.2 compares the proportion of inmates and civilians enumerated in nonmetropolitan areas. The differences are quite striking. Between 2006 and 2008, 16.7 percent of white and 9.6 percent of black male civilians between the ages of twenty-five and forty-four reported living in a nonmetro area, using the 2000 Census definition. The likelihood of being enumerated in a nonmetro area is two to three times higher among inmates. Over one-third of both black and white inmates living in correctional institutions are enumerated in nonmetro areas.

If we combine the civilian and institutionalized population to construct adjusted estimates of nonmetro enumeration, we find that young black men are significantly more likely to be living in nonmetro areas than conventional data sources imply. Among low-skill men, blacks are more likely to be enu-

Table 6.2   Adjusted and Unadjusted Estimates of Nonmetropolitan Enumeration for Men Ages Twenty to Thirty-Four, by Education, 2006 to 2008

	Civilian	Inmate	Combined
White, less than high school	19.8%	34.5%	20.7%
White, high school/GED	22.4	36.9	22.7
White, some college	13.3	34.2	13.4
White, all	16.7	35.6	17.0
Black, less than high school	14.3	37.8	20.8
Black, high school/GED	12.3	37.0	14.8
Black, some college	6.3	33.2	7.5
Black, all	9.6	36.7	12.4

Source: Author's calculations based on 2006–2008 American Community Survey (U.S. Census Bureau 2010). See methodological appendix for more details.

merated in nonmetro areas than whites. However, a substantial fraction of those men are living in correctional facilities.

Exactly how and where to count inmates is a source of much debate and concern. Cost and efficiency considerations have led the Census Bureau to determine that inmates are counted where they reside in prison or jail. Court decisions have barred the use of statistical adjustment and sampling for the apportionment of seats in the U.S. House of Representatives as recently as 1999 (U.S. Department of Commerce vs. U.S. House, 525 U.S. 316 335–336, 1999). Unlike the federal government, however, states may adjust Census-provided population tallies for congressional redistricting. For example, in Kansas nonresident respondents from military installations and higher education campuses were subtracted from the state's population total, and resident military personnel and college and university students located in Kansas were recorded in the Census blocks of their permanent residences (Kobach 2011, 3). Since the Voting Rights Acts of 1965 and 1975, states have been pressed to redraw congressional districts such that "one person's vote is to be worth as much as another's" (article 1, section 2, U.S. Constitution).

Several states plan to adjust Census-provided population counts to account for concentrations of inmates who hail from districts quite different from those in which they reside while incarcerated. In some cases, states plan to exclude inmates from the population counts used in redistricting, based on the premise that they are not enfranchised and thus should not be considered in determining adherence to the one-person/one-vote standard. In other states, officials plan to adjust Census-provided estimates of population distribution by reallocating prison and jail inmates to the communities in which they lived prior to incarceration. Such an adjustment will situate the political representation of inmates in the communities from which they hail rather than those in which prison and jail facilities are located. The Census Bureau has agreed to expedite the release of detailed geographic data on prison and jail counts from the 2010 Census in order to facilitate such adjustments. Data on the location of prison and jail inmates should be available to state and local authorities for use in congressional redistricting, although at the time this book was completed, it was not yet publicly available to researchers.

The growth in incarceration may affect more than perceptions of American racial geography or political redistricting. It is increasingly recognized that moving prisoners outside of their home communities disrupts family relationships, social networks, and economic contacts (Braman 2004; Comfort 2008). And the destabilizing effects of mass incarceration extend beyond the individuals incarcerated and their families to the institutions that structure America's most disadvantaged communities. Braman (2004, 215) suggests that the shame that adheres to having a family member incarcerated undermines social solidarity, even in institutions, like churches, that "one might expect to be a place for support and solidarity." Braman's respondents report an unwillingness to discuss the incarceration of a family member outside their immediate family.

Clear (2007) has persuasively argued that high rates of incarceration destabilize America's most disadvantaged communities. Introducing the idea of "coercive mobility," Rose and Clear (1998) contend that high rates of incarceration within communities can trigger residential instability, erode local institutions, and undermine a community's capacity for social control. They suggest that, in the long term, high incarceration rates may fuel increases in crime. The empirical evidence on the incarceration-crime link at the community level is relatively limited, but what exists suggests that the relationship may vary over time. For example, using data collected by Ralph Taylor (2001), James Lynch and William Sabol (2004) find that high incarceration rates are linked to lower crime rates. Yet they find mixed evidence of the relationship between incarceration rates and levels of community social control, which may portend higher crime in the future.

Research has also shown that even minor contacts with the criminal justice system can trigger fairly dramatic restrictions on individuals' geographic mobility and undermine social cohesion (Beckett and Herbert 2008, 2009). Locational restrictions can have profoundly disruptive effects, not only for potential criminal contacts but also for connections to other individuals and organizations vital to maintaining families, health, and employment. For example, as Katherine Beckett and Steve Herbert (2008) point out, individuals who have been arrested—but not convicted—for a drug-related offense may be prohibited from entering areas where drug sales and prostitution are believed to be common. As these authors note, "In some cities, the areas from which people may be banned comprise significant parts of the city, including the entire downtown core in which social and legal services are concentrated" (Beckett and Herbert 2008, 14).

LIMITATIONS OF EXISTING DATA

Despite growing attention to the collateral consequences of mass incarceration, research advances are hampered by data limitations. One of the areas in which the study of the effects of incarceration is most constrained by the lack of available data is health. Although there are important historical reasons for the exclusion of inmates from many health-related studies (see, for example, Wang and Wildeman 2011), inconsistency in the association between incarceration and health (Schnittker, Massoglia, and Uggen 2011) suggests the need to collect more and better data to enable researchers to investigate this association.

In general, the health of the American population has improved over the past few decades, yet not all Americans have benefited equally. Racial inequalities in health and mortality in the United States are persistent, and it is commonly observed that blacks have worse health outcomes and higher mortality at younger ages than whites. For example, despite substantial declines in the overall risk of tuberculosis in the United States in recent decades, blacks are eight times more likely to contract this disease than whites, and even black children have an extraordinarily high prevalence of tuberculosis (Centers for Disease Control and Prevention 2004). Research suggests that blacks are also more likely than whites to have hepatitis C (Committee on Infectious Diseases

2000). And while human immunodeficiency virus/acquired immunodeficiency syndrome (HIV/AIDS) ranks as the fifth-leading cause of death nationwide among women and men age twenty-five to forty-four, by 2004 HIV/AIDS infection was the leading cause of death for African American men ages sthirty-five to forty-four and for African American women ages twenty-five to thirty-four (Centers for Disease Control and Prevention 2006).

Relatively little attention is paid to how patterns of institutionalization affect health and how differential levels of incarceration may exacerbate inequalities in measures of morbidity, yet recent studies suggest that the role of the criminal justice system in health outcomes is complex and not easily characterized (for a careful review, see Schnittker et al. 2011). Small local studies and prison intake surveys suggest that inmates and former inmates have exceptionally high rates of a number of communicable diseases such as tuberculosis, hepatitis C, and HIV/AIDS. Although the research is limited, the available estimates are quite startling. Some estimates place the tuberculosis infection rate among prisoners at close to 25 percent, compared with less than 0.01 percent in the general population. Hepatitis C infection rates range from 20 to 40 percent in the penal population, compared to close to 2 percent of the general population. And estimates place the HIV/AIDS infection rate of prisoners ten times higher than that of nonprisoners (Restum 2005).

Imprisonment may have direct implications for health outcomes through infections acquired in prison or jail, especially in the case of communicable diseases such as tuberculosis, hepatitis C, and HIV/AIDS. Criminal confinement places men and women in close proximity with others who are known to be at high risk for those diseases, and even if they themselves are not infected when they are imprisoned, the chances that they will transmit disease unknowingly after their release are thereby increased. Incarceration may also have negative, though indirect, implications for health outcomes by setting men and women on a "trajectory of cumulative disadvantage" (London and Meyers 2006, 413). Evidence suggests that spending time in prison is associated with poor health outcomes among former inmates long after the term of imprisonment has ended (Massoglia 2008).

High rates of incarceration within particular subgroups may also fuel disease transmission outside of prison by increasing the circulation of infected individuals within otherwise healthy communities. High rates of tuberculosis and HIV uniquely characterize African American communities; the prison system has been implicated in racial inequality in rates of HIV/AIDS, and the incarceration of large segments of particular subgroups of the population may have fueled disease transmission among the non-incarcerated (Johnson and Raphael 2009). Even short-term stints in jail have implications for tuberculosis exposure, and probation/parole may influence individuals' use of public health initiatives like needle exchanges. For example, locational restrictions placed on parolees or probationers may cause them to avoid needle exchanges and then inject in unsafe ways (Beckett and Herbert 2009).

Yet research also finds evidence that incarceration has a protective effect on health and that racial inequalities in health outcomes are diminished in prison (Patterson 2010; Binswanger et al. 2007; Binswanger, Krueger, and Steiner 2009). Evelyn Patterson (2010) finds lower risks of mortality among black men in prison compared with similar men who are not incarcerated. Similarly, Ingrid Binswanger and her colleagues (2007) find steep increases in mortality risks immediately after release from prison. Jason Schnittker, Michael Massoglia, and Christopher Uggen (2011) observe that the relationship between incarceration and racial disparities in health outcomes may have to be understood in relation to the societal inequalities that shape health behaviors and access to health care in different sociodemographic groups. For example, inmates may have better health outcomes in prison than outside it because while imprisoned they have a constitutionally protected right to health care, which they might not receive otherwise.

Despite growing evidence that the prison system may itself serve as a vector of preventable disease, little information is readily available to use to examine the implications of the prison system for the health status of inmates, let alone the children, families, and communities most deeply affected by incarceration. Surveys of health status taken to gauge the well-being of the population commonly exclude inmates, and federally administered surveys of the health status of inmates are not always comparable to those conducted with the non-institutionalized population.

For example, table 6.3 compares data on tuberculosis and HIV status collected through the National Health and Nutrition Examination Survey (NHANES) and surveys of inmates conducted by the Bureau of Justice Statistics. Among whites, data show that inmates exhibit slightly greater risks of testing positive for either tuberculosis or HIV than civilians. Among blacks, however, inmates report lower rates of tuberculosis and HIV than estimates generated from the civilian population. The results from these national sur-

Table 6.3   Health Status Measures for Men Ages Twenty-Five to Forty-Four, Mid-2000s

	Non-Institutionalized		Inmates	
	Latent TB	HIV	Latent TB	HIV
White, less than high school	0.0%	0.0%	5.2%	1.2%
White, high school/GED	2.5	0.2	3.2	0.8
White, some college	5.3	0.7	2.6	1.2
White, all	3.9	0.5	4.1	1.0
Black, less than high school	9.8	4.5	6.5	2.3
Black, high school /GED	13.0	3.1	6.7	1.9
Black, some college	8.7	2.6	4.2	1.8
Black, all	10.0	3.3	6.3	2.1

Source: Author's calculations using Surveys of Inmates (U.S. Dept. of Justice, BJS, various years–a, various years–b, and various years–c; U.S. Dept. of Justice, Bureau of Prisons 2004), and National Health and Nutrition Examination Survey (Centers for Disease Control and Prevention, National Center for Health Statistics 2007). See methodological appendix for more details.

veys of inmates contradict those provided by local studies and inmate intake surveys, which typically show much higher rates of tuberculosis and HIV among the inmate population across sociodemographic groups.

According to data from the NHANES for 1999 and 2000, 3.9 percent of white men and 10 percent of black men between the ages of twenty-five and forty-four have ever tested positive for tuberculosis. Positive tuberculosis tests and latent tuberculosis are more common among whites and less common among blacks in the incarcerated population; estimates place rates of latent tuberculosis at 4.9 percent of white inmates and 9.4 percent of black inmates. Data from the NHANES for 1999 through 2006 indicate that 0.5 percent of white men and 3.3 percent of black men between the ages of twenty-five and forty-four have ever tested positive for HIV, the virus that causes AIDS. Rates of HIV infection are substantially higher among white inmates than the white civilian population, but that is not the case among blacks.

Differences in survey methodology may account for some of the discrepancy. The NHANES employs an HIV test to generate estimates of HIV status in the population, but correctional surveys rely on inmate self-reports of HIV status. There are a number of reasons to suspect that inmates either do not know or will not report their HIV status. Inmates with HIV are subject to isolation and discriminatory treatment in some states. In others, there is no guarantee that disclosure of HIV status or any other health condition will result in treatment, so incentives to self-disclose are low.

So while some argue that America's prisons and jails may serve as incubators for preventable communicable diseases like tuberculosis, hepatitis C, and HIV/AIDS, there is little evidence from large-scale, nationally representative studies to evaluate such a claim. Undiagnosed and untreated inmates may expose children, partners, and community members when they are released into society. But just as the prison system constructs obstacles to communication that would promote health-enhancing behaviors (Kramer and Comfort 2011), our national data systems do not provide adequate data to fully understand the health consequences of mass incarceration.

CONCLUSION

As previous chapters have demonstrated, the exclusion of inmates from many of our national data systems undermines claims of black educational, economic, and political progress. This chapter contends that the exclusion of inmates from our national data systems obscures the implications of penal system growth for the health and well-being of children, families, and communities. Although qualitative and ethnographic data provide compelling descriptions of the effects of incarceration, there is little by way of large-scale survey data that could help us fully investigate the effects of incarceration on the well-being of children, families, and communities.

Nonetheless, existing research suggests that penal system growth has ramifications far beyond the lives of inmates and former inmates. Generations of children and the communities in which they live are now affected by the criminal justice system. Penal system growth stunts the economic capacity, civic engagement, and social involvement of a growing fraction of American men. Mothers, extended families, and foster care systems can pick up only some of the slack. Educational institutions are hard-pressed to counterbalance the negative effects of penal expansion. While states increase spending on corrections, investments in K-12 education lag (Pew Research Center on the States 2008). As a consequence, the prospects for prosperity for America's most disadvantaged children are bleak.

The way in which we collect data for social science research, policymaking, and evaluation reveals sorely little about the infiltration of an expanding criminal justice system into the lives of the children of inmates. The questions are quite simple, but the data to answer them are scant. Nonetheless, a growing body of scholarship employing careful fieldwork and innovative statistical methods has begun to sketch out the collateral consequences of mass incarceration for children, families, and communities.

Penal system growth has surely generated gains in public safety. Recent research suggests that between 10 and 25 percent of the decline in crime in recent decades is attributable to the growth in incarceration (see, for example, Useem and Piehl 2008; Western and Pettit 2010). Yet the benefits of historically high incarceration rates may be waning, and growing evidence suggests that the public safety gains accrued through penal expansion exact high costs to the public purse, especially in already disadvantaged communities. Children are left without caregivers and breadwinners while their parents spend time in prison or jail. A stint in a correctional facility further undermines the economic capacity of parents to provide for their children and creates social stigma that undermines engaged parenting. A full account of the effects of mass incarceration on inmates, their children, and their communities, however, will require more and better data than are currently available.

CHAPTER 7

Establishing Justice

> We cannot solve the challenges of our time unless we solve them to-
> gether—unless we perfect our union by understanding that we may
> have different stories, but we hold common hopes; that we may not
> look the same and we may not have come from the same place, but
> we all want to move in the same direction towards a better future for
> our children and our grandchildren.
>
> —Presidential candidate Barack Obama, speech on race,
> Philadelphia, March 18, 2008

Establishing a justice system that would provide equal treatment under a system of laws, free from the tyranny of despots and kings, was a centerpiece of
America's founding. The preamble to the U.S. Constitution declares it. The
Bill of Rights further outlines the rights of individuals—including those accused of crimes—in a society governed by the rule of law. The Fourth Amendment protects against unreasonable searches, the Fifth guarantees protection
against self-incrimination, the Sixth further articulates rights related to criminal prosecutions, and the Eighth provides for protection against cruel and
unusual punishment. Yet for much of U.S. history there was a gulf between
"the illusion and reality" of constitutional protection (Pye 1968).

During the civil rights era, the Supreme Court issued numerous rulings
limiting the power of government over criminal defendants and promising
greater legal protections for individuals accused of crimes. Decisions made by
the Warren Court—Mapp, Gideon, and Miranda among them—recognized

and guaranteed defendants' most basic procedural rights regardless of whether their case was tried in state or federal court (Pye 1968).

Mapp v. Ohio (367 U.S. 643, 1961) prevents prosecutors in state courts from using evidence seized in searches that violate the Fourth Amendment's protection against unreasonable searches and seizures. In Gideon v. Wainwright (372 U.S. 335, 348, 1963), the Supreme Court maintained that the right of indigent defendants in a criminal trial to have the assistance of counsel is a fundamental right essential to a fair trial. Gideon made clear that the right to counsel holds whether a defendant is tried in state or federal court, and whether a defendant is involved in a capital or noncapital case. In Miranda v. Arizona (384 U.S. 436, 1966), the Warren Court asserted that the Fifth Amendment's protections against self-incrimination extend beyond criminal court proceedings. Statements made by individuals during interrogations by law enforcement officers are inadmissible in prosecution unless they comply with the Fifth Amendment's safeguards against self-incrimination.

More recently, the Supreme Court has ruled to protect criminal defendants from the indiscriminate exercise of power by judges or seemingly arbitrary guidelines established by the Federal Sentencing Commission. Blakely v. Washington (542 U.S. 296, 2004), the United States v. Booker (543 U.S. 220, 2005), and United States v. Fanfan (543 U.S. 220, 2005) struck down mandatory federal sentencing guidelines and upheld a criminal defendant's right to a jury trial, expressed in the Sixth Amendment.

Yet there is little cause for optimism. The American criminal justice system continued its record expansion into the twenty-first century, and decades of penal expansion have led to the retrenchment of the rights of citizenship of America's most disadvantaged groups. Others have alleged that practices within the criminal justice system itself undermine the rights of individuals codified by the law and fuel a system of racial inequality (Alexander 2010). Police routinely violate the spirit—if the not the letter—of protections against search and seizure, poor and indigent defendants are not consistently provided counsel, and fewer than one in one hundred criminal defendants are ever tried by a jury of their peers (Alexander 2010).

My argument contends that the contemporary criminal justice system creates a unique form of social exclusion that is rooted in the invisibility of America's inmates. Crime and criminals are the subject of much attention and ire in America's newsrooms and living rooms, yet inmates are effectively hidden from public view. Prisons and jails are often located in sparsely populated communities, out of sight of the majority of Americans living in cities and metropolitan areas. And inmates are excluded from the federal data collection efforts commonly used to generate accounts of the economic, political, and social well-being of the American population, thereby being omitted from consideration in deliberations of social policy and designs of social research.

The acute concentration of incarceration among low-skill black men fuels myths of black progress. To read America's newspapers or listen to the debates that engage federal, state, and local policymakers, one might suspect that African Americans are increasingly likely to be getting ahead economically and becoming engaged politically. Claims of growing racial equality are attributed to educational expansion, economic growth, political mobilization, and legal protections provided by half-century-old civil rights legislation. Social scientists' honed inquiry into the causal effects of incarceration eclipses attention to descriptive accounts of the sheer scale of incarceration and its implications for the establishment of social facts about the U.S. population.

To be sure, there are plenty of examples of well-positioned and well-heeled African Americans, and there are certainly black children who grow up to become more successful than their parents. Perhaps the most notable among them, Barack Obama, built his presidential candidacy around his own rags-to-riches experience of the American Dream. His candidacy resonated with many Americans desperate to believe in a just and color-blind society where hard work and perseverance enable even the most disadvantaged to get ahead.

Incorporating inmates into accounts of American inequality dispels myths of black progress by revealing that decades of penal expansion have concealed continued black disadvantage from public view. Among young black men, including inmates implies a nationwide high school dropout rate more than 40 percent higher than conventional estimates suggest and no improvement in the black-white gap in high school graduation rates since the early 1990s. In 2008, during what has become known as the "Great Recession," black male dropouts were *more* likely to be in prison or jail than to be employed. And incorporating inmates suggests that relative wages among young black men have seen little improvement over the last twenty years. On educational and economic indicators, blacks are not getting ahead. Accounting for mass incarceration suggests that they are, in fact, falling even further behind.

Mass incarceration has also created an illusion of growing democratic engagement among young blacks. Incarceration artificially inflates turnout rates among African American men because inmates are underrepresented in the surveys used to gauge trends in voting. Inmates who are excluded from tallies of voter turnout are the same inmates who are disenfranchised from the vote itself owing to the voting restrictions placed on felons in forty-eight states. As debate swirls around whether inmates would vote if they could, evidence indicates that there has been relatively little change in the levels of democratic engagement of young black men when we consider inmates. Accounting for mass incarceration generates the observation that a similar fraction of young black men voted in the election that featured Barack Obama as the one that pitted Ronald Reagan against Jimmy Carter. Although Obama's charismatic candidacy and political organization may have led to higher turnout rates among eligible voters, an increasing share of young black men was disenfranchised. Upon close examination, there is little support for the contention that the political engagement of young blacks broke records or exceeded that of young white men in the 2008 election.

The effects of mass incarceration are keenly felt by the partners, children, and families of inmates and in the communities in which they lived before and after their periods of incapacitation. One of the greatest risks of mass incarceration is that a new generation of children, especially black children, will be cut off from the promise of the American dream. Children are deprived of the possibility of the economic and social involvement of their parents when those parents are incarcerated. When parents get out of prison, they may unwittingly subject their partner, children, and community to a range of communicable diseases like tuberculosis, HIV/AIDS, and hepatitis C. Prohibitions on ex-felons living in households that receive federal housing assistance may contribute to forced separation even in families that aspire to reunite. The children of inmates are commonly consigned to live in disadvantaged communities with poor schools. In communities with few economic opportunities and low levels of civic engagement, it is hardly surprising to find high levels of intergenerational transmission of incarceration.

THE TIP OF THE ICEBERG

The contemporary American criminal justice system is unique in both historical and cross-national perspective, and its implications for accounts of black progress are profound. Yet inmates represent only the "tip of the iceberg" of socially marginalized individuals who are not well counted or well considered in the design, implementation, and evaluation of American social policy and social science research. Inmates are emblematic of socially isolated groups that draw the ire of the media and the public, yet fall under the radar of federal data collection efforts and social science research. Undocumented immigrants, the unstably housed, veterans, and children involved in the foster care system are other groups that are likely to be systematically underrepresented in data collection efforts that assume a domestic life stably situated in households.

Basic demographic descriptions of those socially marginalized groups are even more elusive than such descriptions of inmates. The number of undocumented immigrants and homeless people is widely disputed, and detailed information about their needs and capacities is primarily limited to local area studies. Analysts agree that accurate counts of those populations require novel data collection or indirect estimation methods, yet considerable disagreement about the size of those groups persists. For example, using data from the Current Population Survey, researchers at the Urban Institute estimated that 9.2 million undocumented immigrants lived in the United States in 2002 (Passel, Capps, and Fix 2004). Jeffrey Passel and D'Vera Cohn (2009) claim that the number of undocumented immigrants peaked at 11.9 million in 2006, but has fallen since. Using different data and an alternative estimation method, Robert Justich and Betty Ng (2005) suggest that closer to 20 million undocumented immigrants live in the United States. Discrepancies on that order certainly deserve further scrutiny.

The number of homeless people in the United States is also a hotly debated question. The U.S. Department of Housing and Urban Development (HUD) (2009) estimates that 664,414 individuals were homeless—sheltered or unsheltered—on any given night in January 2008. About 30 percent of them were chronically homeless. HUD also estimates that as many as 1.6 million individuals spent time in a homeless shelter in a twelve-month period from 2007 to 2008 (HUD 2009). Although now dated, estimates provided by the Urban Institute (2000) are significantly higher and suggest that between 2.3 and 3.5 million people were homeless in a one-year period in the late 1990s. More than one-third of the homeless identified in the Urban Institute study were children.

From data gathered in the 2006 to 2008 American Communities Surveys, the Census Bureau estimates that there are almost 23 million veterans. Although the vast majority of veterans successfully reintegrate into civilian society after their period of service, growing evidence suggests that some veterans experience acute difficulties reintegrating into the economic, political, and social routines of civilian life (see, for example, Uggen 2010). Unlike inmates and other socially marginalized groups, veterans have an expansive institutional apparatus in the form of the Department of Veterans Affairs, which aims to help alleviate the problems of social reintegration that plague them. Nonetheless, many veterans elude the public record, especially the most disadvantaged among them.

According to the most current data provided by the Adoption and Foster Care Analysis and Reporting System, there were approximately 463,000 children in foster care in the United States in September 2008, and nearly 300,000 children enter and leave the foster care system each year (U.S. Department of Health and Human Services 2009). It is unclear what fraction of American children will spend some time in the foster care system or how time in foster care relates to parental incarceration, homelessness, or other aspects of social marginality. In addition, there is some question about how states report on children in the foster care system, and there is evidence to suggest that even greater numbers of children are in the care of someone other than their parent or principal caregiver than DHHS estimates imply.

There is very little data to bring to bear on the question of the extent of overlap among socially marginalized groups. We know that ex-inmates face a high risk of homelessness, that children in the foster care system face a high risk of criminal justice contact, and that many undocumented immigrants are unstably housed. But just what fraction of the homeless population has had contact with the criminal justice system? What fraction of children formerly involved in the foster care system end up in America's prisons or jails? What fraction of people living on streets and in homeless shelters are veterans or undocumented immigrants? Answering these questions will require concerted attention by the research community and involve new data collection and the application of innovative statistical methodology. Researchers' efforts would be aided, of course, by the support of the agencies tasked with providing for the needs of socially marginalized groups and evaluating the effectiveness of programs designed to serve them.

IMPLICATIONS FOR POLICY AND RESEARCH

The findings presented in this book that derive from the exclusion of inmates are not simply a statistical exercise, a foray into fact-checking, or an idle observation. The omission of more than 2.3 million people from national data collection efforts has consequences beyond descriptive assessments of the American experience and the debunking of contemporary myths of black progress. The results have import for the design and evaluation of social policy and social scientific research into the theoretical underpinnings of behavioral processes.

Data from the Census and ongoing federally administered surveys are routinely employed by policymakers and bureaucrats in Washington, D.C., in states, and in localities across the country. The founders mandated periodic data collection on the size and distribution of the population for the purposes of political apportionment. The development of grants-in-aid in the 1860s was associated with more extensive data collection efforts to determine the needs and capacities of the nation's inhabitants. The two periods in the twentieth century that witnessed the greatest shifts in redistribution of federal resources to states and localities accompanied seismic shifts in federal data collection efforts. The New Deal era of the 1930s led to the routine collection of data on the needs and capacities of the population through surveys that employed household-based sampling. Sample surveys of the non-institutionalized population proliferated in the 1960s during and immediately following the Johnson administration.

Even today, policymakers and social scientists continue to rely on sampling designs initiated in the 1930s, despite the weight of evidence that undermines confidence in claims derived from them. From the Obama administration's calls for data-driven decision-making to the requirements of congressional apportionment and redistricting, to lawmakers' use of population estimates to design and evaluate a host of social programs, better data are needed to represent the full range of American experiences. Only time will tell if the "Great Recession" of the late 2000s induces the kind of redistributive policies and federal revenue-sharing that characterized the New Deal era of the 1930s or the Great Society programs of the 1960s. If it does, perhaps these policies will also be accompanied by a significant rethinking of how we collect data about the population and its needs and capacities in order to most effectively design and evaluate social programs.

There is ample room to revise our national data systems in ways that better represent the fullness of the American experience. We might begin by acknowledging the limitations of surveys limited to the household population in ways that have been articulated in this book. The Current Population Survey and others like it may be useful for economists who want to gauge slack in the labor market as measured by the unemployment rate. They may be useful for political parties interested in finding and tapping into veins of eligible voters who have failed to turn out in elections. Yet these surveys misrepresent trends over time in any measure of the population that is linked to gender, race, and education simply because the composition of Americans living in households has changed over time in ways that are deeply connected to inequality in America. The penal system now siphons more than 2.3 million disadvantaged Americans out of households and out of consideration for most federally administered surveys. Consequently, our national data systems and the social facts they produce are fundamentally flawed.

Surveys could, of course, do a better job of incorporating inmates. Sampling frames could be expanded to include inmates living in prisons or jails. Surveys could consistently ask more detailed questions about contact with the criminal justice system in order to gauge the extent of sample bias induced by prison growth or the omission of inmates and former inmates from a given survey. Parallel surveys of the household and institutionalized populations could be conducted to facilitate the combining of estimates to construct more representative portraits of Americans living in different environments. Yet those methods do not solve similar problems of exclusion for other socially marginalized groups—such as children in the foster care system, veterans, the unstably housed, and undocumented immigrants—who may have tangential connections to households.

Our national data collection efforts require fundamental rethinking to accommodate the experiences of socially marginalized groups. Researchers have made great strides in using new methods like respondent-driven sampling to find and interview members of traditionally marginalized groups, such as IV drug users and commercial sex workers. Administrative data have shed light on the myriad ways in which children in the foster care system, for example, intersect with numerous state agencies. And more than one hundred years after the pioneering work of W. E. B. DuBois and others, ethnographers continue to conduct careful fieldwork that documents the economic, political, and social lives of men, women, and children who are overlooked by conventional data collection methods. Yet even with their strengths, each of these methods also carries weaknesses. A concerted effort on the part of America's most careful thinkers is warranted.

Acute sample bias associated with the exclusion of socially marginal groups from sample surveys has profound implications for social science research.

Social scientists' obsession with causally oriented research has led to growing investments in trying to identify the consequences of mass incarceration at the expense of attention to the descriptive features of the criminal justice system. Any criminologist can tell you that the size of the penal population has grown, but few know—or have thought about—how the exclusion of inmates from surveys of the population biases estimates of the effects of education on, for example, employment or earnings. As pointed out in chapter 5, the education gap in voting is smaller for blacks than for whites, leading scholars to suspect that organizations like the black church and political parties have been more effective for black turnout than for white turnout. It is quite likely that low-skill blacks who answer surveys are very different from low-skill blacks generally. The sample selection effects induced by mass incarceration, then, not only distort statistics on the turnout rate but also confound explanations for turnout. Similar problems plague causally oriented research on educational attainment, employment, family formation, and a host of other outcomes.

Perhaps even more problematic, however, is that incarceration is so common in some sociodemographic groups that there are few comparable individuals in the population who have not experienced incarceration. The ubiquity of incarceration among low-skill black men undercuts research designs that require comparison groups to isolate the effects of incarceration from other factors like race, low education, or living in disadvantaged neighborhoods. A significant body of causally oriented research on the effects of incarceration uses quasi-experimental designs or methods that compare the outcomes of inmates or former inmates with similarly situated individuals who have not been to prison or jail. There is no valid comparison group for many of America's inmates exactly because incarceration now inheres in whole sociodemographic groups, making it increasingly difficult to identify the effect of incarceration. Cross-national research designs may be promising but are not without limitations.

CONCLUSION

The constitutional mandate to take a decennial census has shaped over two hundred years of data gathering and established the foundation for modern data collection efforts. Émile Durkheim's (1895/1982) pioneering work on the establishment and explanation of social facts has framed more than a century of social scientific research. In just three decades, the criminal justice system has expanded so extensively, yet become concentrated so intensively among low-skill black men, that it compromises the usefulness of data intended for the design and evaluation of social policy and undermines the establishment of social facts and their explanation.

There are certainly alternatives to incarceration. During a time of growing fiscal constraint, states are revisiting expensive custodial sentences for nonviolent or low-level drug and property offenders. Intensive community-based supervision, drug treatment programs, and other alternatives to incarceration are attracting attention. But, as the founders so clearly articulated in the constitutional mandate to collect data on the population, good governance demands good data about the population, its needs, and its capacities. Well-designed social policy, criminal justice–related and otherwise, demands better data on America's most disadvantaged.

Only by paying careful attention to the descriptive contours of incarceration and incorporating inmates into conventional accounts of the population do we have enough information to begin an inquiry into its causes and effects. If we hope to understand the prospects for progress among African Americans, we need to rethink our data collection systems. The increase in incarceration rates has widespread effects, but it is my contention that if we use existing data, we cannot yet measure them well. The concentration of criminal justice contact and incarceration among low-skill, black men makes it incredibly difficult to use tools now common in social science research to explain its buildup or its effects. There is little doubt, however, that the causes of the prison buildup have little to do with crime or that its effects are not limited to those who spend time behind bars.

Mass incarceration is itself a social fact, inhering in a social group, quite apart from the actions or characteristics of any individual within that group. Exactly how to best incorporate inmates and other socially marginalized groups into accounts of the American population is not entirely clear. Only by confronting the full extent of the effects of mass incarceration on even the most basic measures of the U.S. population can we begin to understand its implications.

METHODOLOGICAL APPENDIX

CHAPTER 1

I begin by constructing estimates of the number of persons incarcerated by sex, race, age, and education from 1980 to 2008. To obtain these estimates I use aggregate data on penal populations from the Bureau of Justice Statistics (BJS). Aggregated data for the entire time series are available by facility type, not for specific sex, race-ethnicity, age, and education groups. Data on inmate totals come from the Sourcebook of Criminal Justice Statistics Online (http://www.albany.edu/sourcebook/pdf/t612006.pdf), "Prison Inmates at Mid-Year 2008," and "Jail Inmates at Mid-Year 2008." Data for federal and state inmates from 1982 to 1984 and 1986 to 1989 are provided by BJS. Jail counts are for the last business day in June, and state and federal counts are for December 31—except in 2007 and 2008, when they are also in June.

Microdata from correctional surveys are used to estimate proportions of inmates within sex, race-ethnicity, age, and education groups. Surveys used include the Survey of Inmates of Local Jails (SILJ) (U.S. Dept. of Justice, Bureau of Justice Statistics, various years–b; 1978, 1983, 1989, 1996, 2002), the Survey of Inmates of State Correctional Facilities (SISCF; U.S. Dept. of Justice, Bureau of Justice Statistics, various years–a; 1979, 1986, 1991, 1997, 2004), and the Survey of Inmates of Federal Correctional Facilities (SIFCF; U.S. Dept. of Justice, Bureau of Justice Statistics, various years–c; 1991, 1997, 2004). I interpolate between survey years (within facility type). The estimates for federal inmates prior to 1991 are calculated based on the 1991 SIFCF distributions. Estimates for inmates after the last survey year (2002 for SILJ, 2004 for SISCF, and 2004 for SIFCF) are calculated based on survey distributions in the last survey.

The analysis reports incarceration rates of men age twenty to thirty-four by race and educational attainment. The "civilian incarceration rate" represents the proportion of the U.S. civilian population that is incarcerated. Civilian population totals come from combining estimates of the civilian population from the March Current Population Survey (CPS; U.S. Census Bureau, various years) with estimates of the inmate population. For more details on the construction of estimates or for additional tables of incarceration rates by year, see Pettit, Sykes, and Western (2009).

Table 1.4 reports the cumulative risk of incarceration by age thirty to thirty-four cross-tabulated by sex, race, and educational attainment for cohorts born from 1945 to 1949 through 1975 to 1979. Calculations for the cumulative risk of imprisonment require age-specific first-incarceration and mortality rates. The age-specific first-incarceration rate is the number of people of a given age entering prison for the first time, divided by the number of people of that age in the population at risk. Estimating age-specific risks of first incarceration requires: (1) the number of people in a given age group annually admitted to prison for the first time, (2) the sum total of surviving inmates and ex-inmates in that age group admitted in earlier years, and (3) a population count of those in the age group. These quantities are used to calculate the age-specific risks of first incarceration in a given year. The probabilities of incarceration are then used to calculate the number of incarcerations occurring in the population. The cumulative risk of incarceration is the sum of incarcerations over the initial population.

The number of first-time prison admissions for a given sociodemographic subgroup is not directly observed but is estimated by using microdata from correctional surveys of state and federal inmates conducted between 1974 and 2004. Intersurvey years are interpolated to provide annual estimates. Because estimates of the proportion of first admissions are based on survey data recorded at a single point in time, inmates incarcerated less than a year are undercounted. Information about brief stays is incorporated with data from the National Corrections Reporting Program (NCRP). NCRP data are used to calculate an adjustment factor, which is a function of the fraction of brief prison stays estimated to have been missed by the inmate surveys. Mortality data to form the survival rates are taken from life tables published in *Vital Statistics for the United States* by the National Center for Health Statistics. Population counts are taken from Census enumerations and projections provided by the Census Bureau Population Estimates Program.

Cumulative risks of imprisonment are estimated for three levels of education: less than high school, high school diploma/GED, and some college. Population counts come from inter-Census population estimates weighted by the incarceration-adjusted CPS educational distribution (see the notes to chapter 3 later in this appendix for further discussion of the CPS education adjustment). Although I take age-specific mortality rates from published mortality tables, I adjust for differential mortality by education using figures from the National Longitudinal Mortality Study (NLMS), which reports mortality by education. These figures are used to calculate multipliers for each sex-race-age group to approximate education-specific mortality rates.

These methods of calculating the lifetime risks of imprisonment differ from those used to generate estimates in Western (2006) and Pettit and Western (2004), in two ways. First, I include newly available and revised data whenever possible. Second, I do not adjust the age-specific first-incarceration rates to account for prior incarceration. Employing the exact methodology outlined in Western (2006) and Pettit and Western (2004) generates lifetime risks of incarceration among recent cohorts of low-skill black men that exceed one, owing to extremely high rates of incarceration among low-skill black men, small population sizes (and likely undercount), and the use of five-year intervals for estimation.

The estimates reported here are somewhat lower than those reported in previous work (Pettit and Western 2004; Western 2006). Nonetheless, consistent with previous work, these results point to important differences in the risk of imprisonment across sociodemographic groups and significant growth in the risk of imprisonment over time (and cohorts).

CHAPTER 3

Table 3.1 shows incarceration rates using up to six different estimation strategies. Two are derived exclusively from Census data. "Census institutionalized" represents the proportion of the population that is institutionalized as reported in the decennial Census or the American Community Survey (ACS; U.S. Census Bureau 2010). There is evidence that the number of institutionalized is not a good proxy for incarceration in the early years of prison expansion (1980) and that the ACS underestimates the institutionalized in the most recent years.

I am able to specifically identify prison and jail inmates in only one Census year (1980). The proportion incarcerated using that information is in the row labeled "Census corrections."

Additional estimates are generated using data from the BJS on inmate counts combined with population estimates provided by the Census or population estimates generated by using March CPS data with survey weights. "Census education" estimates use educational distributions from the Census and ACS. "CPS education" estimates use educational distributions from the March CPS.

There is evidence that both the Census and the CPS generate overly optimistic accounts of the educational distribution of the population, particularly within sociodemographic groups with high incarceration rates. Although the reasons for this are complex, it is likely that individuals with low levels of education are systematically undercounted in the Census and missed in surveys like the CPS and ACS. The exclusion of military and institutionalized persons from the CPS also contributes to overly optimistic accounts of the educational attainment of black men.

Therefore, I construct a series where I "adjust" CPS educational distributions to include those living in prisons and jails (for more on the rationale for this, see chapter 4). "CPS adjusted education" estimates adjust CPS educational distributions to include inmates. Unfortunately, I do not have information on other groups not included in the CPS (other military in households and in group quarters or people living in noncorrectional institutions).

Finally, I construct a series of civilian incarceration rates in which I use weighted population totals from the March CPS adjusted to include inmates. The results throughout the book are based on the civilian incarceration rates shown in row 6 of table 3.1.

CHAPTERS 4 AND 5

To obtain estimates of adjusted educational attainment, employment-population ratios, wage gaps, and inequality in voter turnout, I replicate analyses that I have conducted in other publications. For additional methodological details with respect to each specific measure, please see Western and Pettit (2010) and Western and Pettit (2000) on employment; Western and Pettit (2005) and Pettit, Sykes, and Western (2009) on wages; Ewert, Sykes, and Pettit (2010) on education; and Rosenfeld, Laird, Sykes, and Pettit (2010) on voter turnout. Each analysis combines existing data on non-institutionalized household populations with aggregate data on penal populations from the Bureau of Justice Statistics and microdata from surveys of inmates.

CHAPTER 6

Table 6.1 shows the percentage of children who have ever had a parent in prison, cross-tabulated by the child's race and the educational attainment of the incarcerated parent. I estimate the cumulative risk of parental imprisonment for children by race-ethnicity and parental educational attainment for cohorts born since 1960 to 1964, making slight adjustments to methods outlined in Wildeman (2009). Similar to the estimation of the risk of incarceration among adults outlined earlier, calculations for the cumulative risk of parental imprisonment require age-specific incarceration and mortality rates. The age-specific incarceration rate is the number of children of a given age with a parent entering prison for the first time since the child's birth, divided by the number of children of that age in the population at risk. Estimating age-specific risks of parental incarceration requires: (1) the number of children in a given age group annually with a parent admitted to prison in the last year and for the first time since the child's birth, (2) the sum total of surviving children in that age group with parents admitted in earlier years, and (3) a population count of children in the age group. These quantities are used to calculate the age-specific risks of parental incarceration in a given year. The probabilities of incarceration are then used to calculate the number of incarcerations occurring in the population. The cumulative risk of incarceration is the sum of incarcerations over the initial population.

I use microdata from correctional surveys of state and federal inmates conducted between 1974 and 2004 to estimate prison admissions. I construct estimates of the number of children within given age groups (zero to four, five to nine, ten to fourteen, fifteen to seventeen) whose parent was incarcerated in the last year and for the first time since the child's birth. I adjust microdata-generated estimates of the number of children experiencing parental imprisonment for the first time to account for prison growth over the year using data on aggregate penal population counts provided by the BJS and unobserved short stays provided by the National Corrections Reporting Program. Intersurvey years are interpolated to provide annual estimates. Mortality data to form the survival rates are taken from life tables published in *Vital Statistics in the United States* by the National Center for Health Statistics. Population counts are taken from Census enumerations and projections provided by the

Census Bureau Population Estimates Program. Following Wildeman (2009), I use the Natality Detail File from the National Vital Statistics Registry to generate the educational distributions of parents of children of different birth cohorts.

Figure 6.1 reports the number of children with a parent in prison or jail using microdata from correctional surveys (listed earlier). Following Glaze and Maruschak (2008), I first estimate the number of parents in prison or jail who had minor children by applying the distribution of parents found in correctional surveys to aggregate data on penal population counts from the BJS. For each year, I multiply the estimated number of parents by gender and race by the number of minor children reported by male and female inmates. The estimates are then summed by gender and reported as totals. Children are assigned the race-ethnicity of their incarcerated parent.

REFERENCES

Alexander, Michelle. 2010. *The New Jim Crow: Mass Incarceration in the Age of Color-blindness.* New York: New Press.

American National Election Studies (ANES). 2005. "The ANES Guide to Public Opinion and Electoral Behavior, Voter Turnout 1948–2008." Table 6A.2.2. Available at: http://www.electionstudies.org/nesguide/2ndtable/t6a_2_2.htm (accessed July 27, 2010).

Anderson, Margo. 1988. *The American Census: A Social History.* New Haven, Conn.: Yale University Press.

Anderson, Margo, and Stephen Fienberg. 1999. *Who Counts: The Politics of Census-Taking in Contemporary America.* New York: Russell Sage Foundation.

Andrews, Kenneth. 1997. "The Impacts of Social Movements on the Political Process: The Civil Rights Movement and Black Electoral Politics in Mississippi." *American Sociological Review* 62(5): 800–819.

Apel, Robert, and Gary Sweeten. 2010. "The Impact of Incarceration on Employment During the Transition to Adulthood." *Social Problems* 57(3): 448–79.

Arditti, Joyce, Jennifer Lambert-Shute, and Karen Joest. 2003. "Saturday Morning at the Jail: Implications of Incarceration for Families and Children." *Family Relations* 52(3): 195–204.

Arum, Richard, and Irenee Beattie. 1999. "High School Experience and the Risk of Adult Incarceration." *Criminology* 37(3): 515–40.

Arum, Richard, and Gary LaFree. 2008. "Educational Attainment, Teacher-Student Ratios, and the Risk of Adult Incarceration Among U.S. Birth Cohorts Since 1910." *Sociology of Education* 81(4): 397–421.

Ashenfelter, Orley, William Collins, and Albert Yoon. 2006. "Evaluating the Role of *Brown v. Board of Education* in School Equalization, Desegregation, and the Income of African Americans." *American Law and Economics Review* 8(2): 213–48.

Beck, Allen, and Paige Harrison. 2006. "Prison and Jail Inmates at Midyear, 2005." National Criminal Justice Archive 213133. Washington: U.S. Department of Justice.

Beckett, Katherine. 1997. *Making Crime Pay: Law and Order in Contemporary American Politics.* New York: Oxford University Press.

Beckett, Katherine, and Steve Herbert. 2008. "Dealing with Disorder: Social Control in the Post-Industrial City." *Theoretical Criminology* 12(1): 5–30.

———. 2009. *Banished: The New Social Control in Urban America.* New York: Oxford University Press.

Binswanger, Ingrid A., Patrick M. Krueger, and John F. Steiner. 2009. "Prevalence of Chronic Medical Conditions Among Jail and Prison Inmates in the USA Compared with the General Population." *Journal of Epidemiology and Community Health* 63: 912–19.

Binswanger, Ingrid A., Marc F. Stern, Richard A. Deyo, Patrick J. Heagerty, Allen Cheadle, Joann G. Elmore, and Thomas D. Koepsell. 2007. "Release from Prison: A High Risk of Death for Former Inmates." *New England Journal of Medicine* 356: 157–65.

Blank, Rebecca. 2001. "An Overview of Trends in Social and Economic Well-Being by Race." In *America Becoming: Racial Trends and Their Consequences*, vol. 1, edited by Neil Smelser, William Julius Wilson, and Faith Mitchell. Washington, D.C.: National Academies Press.

Blau, Peter, and Otis Dudley Duncan. 1967. *The American Occupational Structure.* New York: Wiley.

Blumstein, Alfred, and Jacqueline Cohen. 1973. "A Theory of the Stability of Punishment." *Journal of Criminal Law and Criminology* 64(2): 198–206.

Bonczar, Thomas. 2003. "Prevalence of Imprisonment in the U.S. Population, 1974–2001." National Criminal Justice Archive 197976. Washington: U.S. Department of Justice.

Bosworth, Mary, and Emma Kaufman. 2011. "Foreigners in a Carceral Age: Immigration and Imprisonment in the U.S." *Stanford Law and Policy Review* 22(1). Oxford Legal Studies Research Paper 34/2011. Available at SSRN: http://ssrn.com/abstract=1852196 (accessed February 1, 2012).

Bound, John, and Richard Freeman. 1992. "What Went Wrong? The Erosion of

Relative Earnings and Employment of Young Black Men in the 1980s." *Quarterly Journal of Economics* 107(1): 201–32.

Bowles, Samuel, and Herbert Gintis. 1976. *Schooling in Capitalist America*. New York: Basic Books.

Braman, Donald. 2004. *Doing Time on the Outside: Incarceration and Family Life in Urban America*. Ann Arbor: University of Michigan Press.

Brown, Lawrence, James Fossett, and Kenneth Palmer. 1984. *The Changing Politics of Federal Grants*. Washington, D.C.: Brookings Institution.

Bulmer, Martin, Kevin Bales, and Kathryn Kish-Sklar, eds. 1991. *The Social Survey in Historical Perspective, 1880–1940*. Cambridge: Cambridge University Press.

Burch, Traci. 2010. "Turnout and Party Registration Among Criminal Offenders in the 2008 General Election." *Law and Society Review* 45(3): 699–730.

Cahill, Edward. 1974. "Migration and the Decline of the Black Population in Rural and Non-Metropolitan Areas." *Phylon* 35(3): 284–92.

California Department of Corrections (CDC). 1997. "Preventing Parolee Failure Program: An Evaluation." National Criminal Justice Archive 180542. Sacramento: CDC.

Cancio, A. Silvia, T. David Evans, and David Maume. 1996. "Reconsidering the Declining Significance of Race: Racial Differences in Early Career Wages." *American Sociological Review* 61(4): 541–56.

Centers for Disease Control and Prevention (CDC). 2004. "Racial Disparities in Tuberculosis—Selected Southern States, 1991–2002." *Morbidity and Mortality Weekly Report* (*MMWR*). Atlanta: CDC.

———. 2006. "Cases of HIV Infection and AIDS in the United States, by Race/Ethnicity, 2000–2004." *HIV/AIDS: Surveillance Supplemental Report* 12(1): 136. Available at: www.cdc.gov/hiv/topics/surveillance/resources/reports/index.htm (accessed March 16, 2012).

Centers for Disease Control and Prevention (CDC), National Center for Health Statistics (NCHS). 2007. *National Health and Nutrition Examination Survey Data, 1999–2006* [Computer files]. Hyattsville, Md.: U.S. Department of Health and Human Services, Centers for Disease Control and Prevention.

Child Trends. 2003. "High School Dropout Rates: The Gap Narrows Between Blacks and Whites." Washington, D.C.: Child Trends (June 16). Available at: http://www.childtrends.org/_mediarelease_page.cfm?LID=FA8D14E2-42ED-4C22-B408FDC3CBF46A53 (accessed September 15, 2010).

Chiricos, Ted, Sarah Eschholz, and Marc Gertz. 1997. "Crime, News, and Fear of

Crime: Toward an Identification of Audience Effects." *Social Problems* 44(3): 342–57.

Citro, Constance, Daniel Cork, and Janet Norwood, eds. 2004. *The 2000 Census: Counting Under Adversity.* Washington, D.C.: National Academies Press.

Clear, Todd. 2007. *Imprisoning Communities: How Mass Incarceration Makes Disadvantaged Neighborhoods Worse.* New York: Oxford University Press.

Comfort, Megan. 2008. *Doing Time Together: Love and Family in the Shadow of the Prison.* Chicago: University of Chicago Press.

Committee on Infectious Diseases (CID). 2000. "Hepatitis C." In *2000 Red Book: Report of the Committee on Infectious Diseases*, 25th ed., edited by L. K. Pickering et al. Elk Grove, Ill.: American Academy of Pediatrics.

Converse, Jean. 1987. *Survey Research in the United States: Roots and Emergence, 1890–1960.* Berkeley: University of California Press.

Crutchfield, Robert. 1989. "Labor Stratification and Violent Crime." *Social Forces* 68(2): 489–512.

Crutchfield, Robert, and Susan Pitchford. 1997. "Work and Crime: The Effects of Labor Stratification on Criminality." *Social Forces* 76(1): 93–118.

Darity, William. 1980. "Illusions of Black Economic Progress." *Review of Black Political Economy* 10(2): 153–68.

Dommel, Paul. 1974. *The Politics of Revenue Sharing.* Bloomington: Indiana University Press.

Donohue, John. 2009. "Assessing the Relative Benefits of Incarceration: Overall Changes and the Benefits on the Margin." In *Do Prisons Make Us Safer? The Benefits and Costs of the Prison Boom*, edited by Steven Raphael and Michael Stoll. New York: Russell Sage Foundation.

Dowler, Kenneth. 2003. "Media Consumption and Public Attitudes Toward Crime and Justice: The Relationship Between Fear of Crime, Punitive Attitudes, and Perceived Police Effectiveness." *Journal of Criminal Justice and Popular Culture* 10(2): 109–26.

Dunaway, Wilma. 2003. *The African American Family in Slavery and Emancipation.* New York: Cambridge University Press.

Durkheim, Émile. 1982. *The Rules of the Sociological Method and Selected Texts on Sociology and Its Method*, edited by Steven Lukes and translated by W. D. Halls. New York: Free Press. (Originally published in 1895.)

Duster, Troy. 1997. "Pattern, Purpose, and Race in the Drug War." In *Crack in America*, edited by Craig Reinarman and Harry Levine. Berkeley: University of California Press.

Edelman, Marian Wright. 1992. *The Measure of Our Success: A Letter to My Children and Yours.* Boston: Beacon Press.

Edin, Kathryn, and Maria Kefalas. 2005. *Promises I Can Keep: Why Poor Women Put Motherhood Before Marriage.* Berkeley: University of California Press.

Edin, Kathryn, Timothy Nelson, and Rechelle Paranal. 2004. "Fatherhood and Incarceration as Potential Turning Points in the Criminal Careers of Unskilled Men." In *Imprisoning America: The Social Effects of Mass Incarceration*, edited by Mary Pattillo, David Weiman, and Bruce Western. New York: Russell Sage Foundation.

Ellison, Ralph. 1952. *Invisible Man.* New York: Random House.

Ewert, Stephanie, Bryan Sykes, and Becky Pettit. 2010. "The Degree of Disadvantage: Incarceration and Racial Inequality in Education." Paper presented to the annual meeting of the Population Association of America. Dallas (April 15–17).

Filer, John, Lawrence Kenny, and Rebecca Morton. 1991. "Voting Laws, Educational Policies, and Minority Turnout." *Journal of Law and Economics* 34: 371–94.

Fischer, Claude, Michael Hout, Martin Sanchez Jankowski, Samuel Lucas, Ann Swidler, and Kim Voss. 1996. *Inequality by Design: Cracking the Bell Curve Myth.* Princeton, N.J.: Princeton University Press.

Foster, Holly, and John Hagan. 2007. "Incarceration and Intergenerational Social Exclusion." *Social Problems* 54(4): 399–433.

Franklin, Donna. 1997. *Ensuring Inequality: The Structural Transformation of the African-American Family.* New York: Oxford University Press.

Freedman, David A. 1991. "Statistical Models and Shoe Leather." *Sociological Methodology* 21: 291–313.

Freeman, Richard, and William Rodgers III. 2000. "Area Economic Conditions and the Labor Market Outcomes of Young Men in the 1990s Expansion." In *Prosperity for All? The Economic Boom and African Americans*, edited by Robert Cherry and William Rogers. New York: Russell Sage Foundation.

Freudenberg, Nicholas. 2001. "Jails, Prisons, and the Health of Urban Populations: A Review of the Impact of the Correctional System on Community Health." *Journal of Urban Health* 78(2): 214–35.

Gamoran, Adam. 2001. "American Schooling and Educational Inequality: A Forecast for the Twenty-First Century." *Sociology of Education* 74: 135–53.

Gamoran, Adam, Marin Nystrand, Mark Berends, and Paul LePore. 1995. "An Organizational Analysis of the Effects of Ability Grouping." *American Educational Research Journal* 32(4): 687–715.

Garland, David. 1990. *Punishment and Modern Society: A Study in Social Theory.* Chicago: University of Chicago Press.

———. 2001. *The Culture of Control: Crime and Social Order in Contemporary Society.* Chicago: University of Chicago Press.

Geller, Amanda, Carey Cooper, Irwin Garfinkel, O. Schwartz-Soicher, and Ronald Mincy. Forthcoming. "Beyond Absenteeism: Father Incarceration and Child Development." *Demography.*

Geller, Amanda, Irwin Garfinkel, Carey E. Cooper, and Ronald D. Mincy. 2009. "Parental Incarceration and Child Well-Being: Implications for Urban Families." *Social Science Quarterly* 90(5): 1186–1202.

Geller, Amanda, Irwin Garfinkel, and Bruce Western. 2011. "Paternal Incarceration and Support for Children in Fragile Families." *Demography* 48(1): 25–47.

Gerber, Alan, and Donald Green. 2000. "The Effects of Canvassing, Telephone Calls, and Direct Mail on Voter Turnout: A Field Experiment." *American Political Science Review* 94(3): 653–63.

Ghosh, Palash R. 2006. "Private Prisons Have a Lock on Growth." *Business Week,* July 6. Available at: http://www.businessweek.com/investor/content/jul2006/pi20060706_849785.htm.

Glaze, Lauren, and Thomas Bonczar. 2008. "Probation and Parole in the United States: 2007 Statistical Tables." National Criminal Justice Archive 224707. Washington: U.S. Department of Justice.

Glaze, Lauren, and Laura M. Maruschak. 2008. "Parents in Prison and Their Minor Children." National Criminal Justice Archive 222984. Washington: U.S. Department of Justice.

Goffman, Alice. 2009. "On the Run: Wanted Men in a Philadelphia Ghetto." *American Sociological Review* 74(3): 339–57.

Goldin, Claudia, and Lawrence Katz. 2008. *The Race Between Education and Technology.* Cambridge, Mass.: Harvard University Press.

Government Accountability Office (GAO). 2005. "Military Personnel: Reporting Additional Servicemember Demographics Could Enhance Congressional Oversight." GAO-05-952. Washington: GAO.

Green, Donald, Alan Gerber, and David Nickerson. 2003. "Getting Out the Vote in Local Elections: Results from Six Door-to-Door Canvassing Experiments." *Journal of Politics* 65(4): 1083–96.

Greene, Jay. 2002. "High School Graduation Rates in the United States." Report. New York: Manhattan Institute for Policy Research.

Greene, Jay, and Marcus Winters. 2006. "Leaving Boys Behind: Public High School Graduation Rates." New York: Manhattan Institute for Policy Research.

Grodsky, Eric, and Devah Pager. 2001. "The Structure of Disadvantage: Individual and Occupational Determinants of the Black-White Wage Gap." *American Sociological Review* 66(4): 542–67.

Gutman, Herbert. 1976. *The Black Family in Slavery and Freedom, 1750–1925.* New York: Vintage.

Hagan, John, and Ronit Dinovitzer. 1999. "Collateral Consequences of Imprisonment for Children, Communities, and Prisoners." *Crime and Justice* 26: 121–62.

Hahn, Steven. 2003. *A Nation Under Our Feet: Black Political Struggles in the Rural South from Slavery to the Great Migration.* Cambridge, Mass.: Harvard University Press.

Hallinan, Maureen. 1994. "Tracking: From Theory to Practice." *Sociology of Education* 67(2): 79–84.

Hanley, Eric. 2001. "Centrally Administered Mobility Reconsidered: The Political Dimension of Educational Stratification in State-Socialist Czechoslovakia." *Sociology of Education* 74(1): 25–43.

Hawkins, Darnell. 2011. "Things Fall Apart: Revisiting Race and Ethnic Differences in Criminal Violence Amidst a Crime Drop." *Race and Justice* 1(1): 3–48.

Heckman, James, and Paul LaFontaine. 2010. "The American High School Graduation Rate: Trends and Levels." *Review of Economics and Statistics* 92(2): 244–62.

Heyer, Rose, and Peter Wagner. 2004. *Too Big to Ignore: How Counting People in Prisons Distorted Census 2000.* Northampton, Mass.: Prison Policy Initiative, Prisoners of the Census (April).

Holzer, Harry, and Paul Offner. 2006. "Trends in the Employment Outcomes of Young Black Men, 1979–2000." In *Black Males Left Behind*, edited by Ron Mincy. Washington, D.C.: Urban Institute Press.

Hout, Michael, Adrian Raftery, and Eleanor Bell. 1993. "Making the Grade: Educational Stratification in the U.S." In *Persistent Inequality: Changing Educational Attainment in Thirteen Countries*, edited by Yossi Shavit and Hans-Peter Blossfeld. Boulder, Colo.: Westview.

International Centre for Prison Studies. 2008. World Prison Brief [searchable database]. Available at: http://www.prisonstudies.org/info/worldbrief (accessed March 13, 2012).

Jacobs, David, and Jason Carmichael. 2002. "The Political Sociology of the Death Penalty: A Pooled Time-Series Analysis." *American Sociological Review* 67(1): 109–23.

Jacobs, David, and Ronald Helms. 1996. "Toward a Political Model of Incarceration: A Time-Series Examination of Multiple Explanations for Prison Admission Rates." *American Journal of Sociology* 102(2): 323–57.

Johnson, Rucker, and Steven Raphael. 2009. "The Effects of Male Incarceration Dynamics on Acquired Immune Deficiency Syndrome Infection Rates Among African American Women and Men." *Journal of Law and Economics* 52: 251–93.

Justich, Robert, and Betty Ng. 2005. "The Underground Labor Force Is Rising to the Surface." New York: Bear Sterns Asset Management (January 3). Available at: http://www.steinreport.com/BearStearnsStudy.pdf (accessed September 15, 2010).

Kain, John. 1971. "Housing Segregation, Negro Employment, and Metropolitan Centralization." *Quarterly Journal of Economics* 26: 110–30.

Kane, Tim. 2005. "Who Bears the Burden? Demographic Characteristics of U.S. Military Recruits Before and After 9/11." Washington, D.C.: Heritage Foundation.

Kasarda, John. 1989. "Urban Industrial Transition and the Underclass." *Annals of the American Academy of Political and Social Science* 501: 26–47.

King, Martin Luther, Jr. 1958. *The Measure of a Man.* Philadelphia: Christian Education Press.

Klite, Paul, Robert Bardwell, and Jason Saltzman. 1997. "Local TV News: Getting Away with Murder." *Harvard International Journal of Press Politics* 2(2): 102–12.

Kobach, Kris. 2011. "Adjustment to the 2010 U.S. Decennial Census." Topeka: Kansas Secretary of State.

Kousser, J. Morgan. 1975. *The Shaping of Southern Politics: Suffrage Restriction and the Establishment of the One-Party South, 1880–1910.* New Haven, Conn.: Yale University Press.

Kozol, Jonathan. 1991. *Savage Inequalities: Children in America's Schools.* New York: Crown.

Kramer, Katie, and Megan Comfort. 2011. "Considerations in HIV Prevention for Women Affected by the Criminal Justice System." *Women's Health Issues* 21(6): S272–77.

Lareau, Annette. 2003. *Unequal Childhoods: Class, Race, and Family Life.* Berkeley: University of California Press.

Lawson, Steven. 1976. *Black Ballots: Voting Rights in the South, 1944–1969.* New York: Columbia University Press.

———. 1985. *In Pursuit of Power: Southern Blacks and Electoral Politics, 1965–1982.* New York: Columbia University Press.

Leighley, Jan, and Arnold Vedlitz. 1999. "Race, Ethnicity, and Political Participation: Competing Models and Contrasting Explanations." *Journal of Politics* 61(4): 1092–1114.

Lemann, Nicholas. 1991. *The Promised Land: The Great Black Migration and How It Changed America*. New York: Vintage.

Liska, Allen, and William Baccaglini. 1990. "Feeling Safe by Comparison: Crime in the Newspaper." *Social Problems* 37(3): 360–74.

Liu, Baodong, Sharon Austin, and Byron Orey. 2009. "Church Attendance, Social Capital, and Black Voting Participation." *Social Science Quarterly* 90(3): 576–92.

Lochner, Lance, and Enrico Moretti. 2004. "The Effect of Education on Crime: Evidence from Prison Inmates, Arrests, and Self-Reports." *American Economic Review* 94(1): 155–89.

London, Andrew, and Nancy Myers. 2006. "Race, Incarceration, and Health: A Life Course Approach." *Research on Aging* 28(3): 409–22.

Lopoo, Leonard, and Bruce Western. 2005. "Incarceration and the Formation and Stability of Marital Unions." *Journal of Marriage and Family* 67(3): 721–34.

Lucas, Samuel. 1999. *Tracking Inequality: Stratification and Mobility in American High Schools*. New York: Teachers College Press.

———. 2001. "Effectively Maintained Inequality: Education Transitions, Track Mobility, and Social Background Effects." *American Journal of Sociology* 106(6): 1642–90.

Lynch, James, and Lynn Addington, eds. 2007. *Understanding Crime Statistics: Revisiting the Divergence of the NCVS and UCR*. New York: Cambridge University Press.

Lynch, James, and Albert Biderman, eds. 1991. *Understanding Crime Incidence Statistics: Why the UCR Diverges from the NCS*. New York: Springer Verlag.

Lynch, James, and William Sabol. 2001. "Prisoner Reentry in Perspective." Crime Policy Report. Washington, D.C.: Urban Institute.

———. 2004. "Effects of Incarceration on Informal Social Control in Communities." In *Imprisoning America: The Social Effects of Mass Incarceration*, edited by Mary Pattillo, David Weiman, and Bruce Western. New York: Russell Sage Foundation.

Lyons, Christopher, and Becky Pettit. 2011. "Compounded Disadvantage: Race, Incarceration, and Wage Growth." *Social Problems* 58(2): 257–80.

Magnusson, Ed. 1981. "The Curse of Violent Crime." *Time*, March 23. Available at: http://www.time.com/time/magazine/article/0,9171,952929,00.html (accessed July 23, 2011).

Manza, Jeff, and Christopher Uggen. 2006. *Locked Out: Felon Disenfranchisement and American Democracy*. New York: Oxford University Press.

Massey, Douglas, and Nancy Denton. 1993. *American Apartheid: Segregation and the Making of the Underclass*. Cambridge, Mass.: Harvard University Press.

Massoglia, Michael. 2008. "Incarceration as Exposure: The Prison, Infectious Disease, and Other Stress-Related Illnesses." *Journal of Health and Social Behavior* 49(1): 57–71.

Mathews, Jay. 2006. "Dropout Data Raise Questions on Two Fronts." *Washington Post*, May 23.

Mauer, Marc. 1994. "Americans Behind Bars: The International Use of Incarceration, 1992–1993: Part 1." Washington, D.C.: The Sentencing Project.

———. 2006. *Race to Incarcerate.* New York: New Press.

McCall, Leslie. 2001. "Sources of Racial Wage Inequality in Metropolitan Labor Markets: Racial, Ethnic, and Gender Differences." *American Sociological Review* 66(4): 520–41.

McDaniel, Antonio. 1995. *Swing Low, Sweet Chariot: The Mortality Cost of Colonizing Liberia in the Nineteenth Century.* Chicago: University of Chicago Press.

McDonald, Michael, and Samuel Popkin. 2001. "The Myth of the Vanishing Voter." *American Political Science Review* 95(4): 963–74.

Miles, Thomas J. 2004. "Felon Disenfranchisement and Voter Turnout." *Journal of Legal Studies* 33: 85–130.

Minton, Todd. 2010. "Jail Inmates at Midyear 2009: Statistical Tables." National Criminal Justice Archive 230122. Washington: U.S. Department of Justice, Office of Justice Programs (June). Available at: http://bjs.ojp.usdoj.gov/content/pub/pdf/jim09st.pdf (accessed October 15, 2011).

Minton, Todd, and William Sabol. 2009. "Jail Inmates at Midyear 2008: Statistical Tables." National Criminal Justice Archive 225709. Washington: U.S. Department of Justice, Office of Justice Programs.

Mishel, Lawrence, and Joydeep Roy. 2006. "Rethinking High School Graduation Rates and Trends." Washington, D.C.: Economic Policy Institute.

Morenoff, Jeffrey, and David Harding. 2011. "Final Technical Report: Neighborhoods, Recidivism, and Employment Among Returning Prisoners." National Criminal Justice Archive 236436. Washington: U.S. Department of Justice. Available at: https://www.ncjrs.gov/pdffiles1/nij/grants/236436.pdf (accessed March 15, 2012).

Morenoff, Jeffrey, David J. Harding, and Amy Cooter. 2009. "The Neighborhood Context of Prisoner Reentry." Paper presented to the annual meeting of the Population Association. Detroit (April 29–May 2).

NAACP Legal Defense and Education Fund. 2007. "Dismantling the School-to-Prison Pipeline." New York: NAACP.

New York Times. 2008. "That's Two for Me" (editorial). November 11.

———. 2010. *New York Times* searchable archive: Various stories with search term "violent crime," 1970–2009. Available at: http://query.nytimes.com/search/ (accessed September 15, 2010).

Nurse, Anne M. 2004. "Returning to Strangers: Newly Paroled Young Fathers and Their Children." In *Imprisoning America: The Social Effects of Mass Incarceration*, edited by Mary Pattillo, David Weiman, and Bruce Western. New York: Russell Sage Foundation.

Orfield, Gary, Daniel Losen, Johanna Wald, and Christopher Swanson. 2004. "Losing Our Future: How Minority Youth Are Being Left Behind by the Graduation Rate Crisis." Cambridge, Mass.: The Civil Rights Project at Harvard University, the Urban Institute, Advocates for Children of New York, and the Civil Society Institute.

Page, Reba. 1991. *Lower Track Classrooms: A Curricular and Cultural Perspective.* New York: Teachers College Press.

Pager, Devah. 2003. "The Mark of a Criminal Record." *American Journal of Sociology* 108(5): 937–75.

———. 2007. *Marked: Race, Crime, and Finding Work in an Era of Mass Incarceration.* Chicago: University of Chicago Press.

Passel, Jeffrey, Randolph Capps, and Michael Fix. 2004. *Undocumented Immigrants: Facts and Figures.* Washington, D.C.: Urban Institute.

Passel, Jeffrey, and D'Vera Cohn. 2009. *A Portrait of Unauthorized Immigrants in the United States 2009.* Washington, D.C.: Pew Hispanic Center.

Patterson, Evelyn. 2010. "Incarcerating Death: Mortality in U.S. State Correctional Facilities, 1985–1998." *Demography* 47(3): 587–607.

Pettit, Becky, Bryan Sykes, and Bruce Western. 2009. "Technical Report on Revised Population Estimates and NLSY-79 Analysis Tables for the Pew Public Safety and Mobility Project." Cambridge, Mass.: Harvard University.

Pettit, Becky, and Bruce Western. 2004. "Mass Imprisonment and the Life Course: Race and Class Inequality in U.S. Incarceration." *American Sociological Review* 69(2): 151–69.

Pew Economic Mobility Project. 2009. "Findings from a National Survey and Focus Groups on Economic Mobility." Washington, D.C.: Pew Charitable Trusts.

Pew Research Center. 2009. "Dissecting the 2008 Electorate: Most Diverse in U.S. History." Washington, D.C.: Pew Charitable Trusts.

Pew Research Center on the States. 2008. "One in 100: Behind Bars in America 2008." Washington, D.C.: Pew Charitable Trusts.

Philpot, Tasha, Daron Shaw, and Ernest McGowen. 2009. "Winning the Race: Black

Voter Turnout in the 2008 Presidential Election." *Public Opinion Quarterly* 73(5): 995–1022.

Pollak, Jessica, and Charis Kubrin. 2007. "Crime in the News: How Crimes, Offenders, and Victims Are Portrayed in the Media." *Journal of Criminal Justice and Popular Culture* 14(1): 59–83.

Preston, Samuel, Irma Elo, Mark Hill, and Ira Rosenwaike. 2003. *The Demography of African Americans, 1930–1990.* Dordrecht, the Netherlands: Kluwer Academic Publishers.

Price, Daniel. 1947. "A Check on Under-enumeration in the 1940 Census." *American Sociological Review* 12(1): 44–49.

Pye, A. Kenneth. 1968. "The Warren Court and Criminal Procedure." *Michigan Law Review* 67(2): 249–68.

Raftery, Adrian, and Michael Hout. 1993. "Maximally Maintained Inequality: Expansion, Reform, and Opportunity in Irish Education, 1921–1975." *Sociology of Education* 66(1): 41–62.

Reid, Herbert. 1982. "Task Force on Violent Crime Report Misses Mark." *Crisis* 89(1): 13–16.

Restum, Zulficar Gregory. 2005. "Public Health Implications of Substandard Correctional Health Care." *American Journal of Public Health* 95(10): 1689–91.

Rhodes, Lorna. 2004. *Total Confinement: Madness and Reason in the Maximum Security Prison.* Berkeley: University of California Press.

Riveland, Chase. 1999. "Supermax Prisons: Overview and General Considerations." National Criminal Justice Archive 177597. Washington: National Institute of Corrections.

Robinson, J. Gregory, Kirsten West, and Arjun Adlakha. 2002. "Coverage of the Population in Census 2000: Results from Demographic Analysis." *Population Research and Policy Review* 21(1–2): 19–38.

Rose, Dina, and Todd Clear. 1998. "Incarceration, Social Capital, and Crime: Implications for Social Disorganization Theory." *Criminology* 36(3): 35–42.

Rosenfeld, Jake, Jennifer Laird, Bryan Sykes, and Becky Pettit. 2010. "Mass Incarceration and Voter Turnout." Paper presented to the annual meeting of the American Society of Criminology. San Francisco (November 17–20).

Rosenfeld, Richard. 2009. "Crime Is the Problem: Homicide, Acquisitive Crime, and Economic Conditions." *Journal of Quantitative Criminology* 25(3): 287–306.

Rosenfeld, Richard, and Stephen Messner. 2009. "The Crime Drop in Comparative Perspective: The Impact of the Economy and Imprisonment on American and European Burglary Rates." *British Journal of Sociology* 60(3): 445–71.

Rusche, Georg, and Otto Kircheimer. 2003. *Punishment and Social Structure.* New York: Transaction Publishers. (Originally published in 1939.)

Sabol, William, Heather West, and Matthew Cooper. 2009. "Prisoners in 2008." National Criminal Justice Archive 228417. *Bureau of Justice Statistics Bulletin* (December). Washington: U.S. Department of Justice, Bureau of Justice Statistics. Available at: http://bjs.ojp.usdoj.gov/content/pub/pdf/p08.pdf (accessed September 16, 2011).

Sacco, Vincent. 1995. "Media Constructions of Crime." *Annals of the American Academy of Political and Social Science* 539: 141–54.

Sakamoto, Arthur, Huei-Hsia Wu, and Jessie M. Tzeng. 2000. "The Declining Significance of Race Among American Men During the Latter Half of the Twentieth Century." *Demography* 37(1): 41–51.

Schnittker, Jason, Michael Massoglia, and Christopher Uggen. 2011. "Incarceration and the Health of the African American Community." *Du Bois Review* 8(1): 133–41.

Sentencing Project. 2010. "Felony Disenfranchisement Laws in the United States." Available at: http://sentencingproject.org/doc/publications/fd_bs_fdlawsinusDec 11.pdf (accessed December 8, 2011).

Shavit, Yossi, and Hans-Peter Blossfeld. 1993. *Persistent Inequality: Changing Educational Attainment in Thirteen Countries.* Boulder, Colo.: Westview.

Siegel, Jacob, and David Swanson. 2004. *The Methods and Materials of Demography.* New York: Academic Press.

Simon, Jonathan. 2007. *Governing Through Crime: How the War on Crime Transformed American Democracy and Created a Culture of Fear.* New York: Oxford University Press.

Snipp, C. Matthew. 1989. *American Indians: The First of This Land.* New York: Russell Sage Foundation.

———. 2003. "Racial Measurement in the American Census: Past Practices and Implications for the Future." *Annual Review of Sociology* 29: 563–88.

Sprott, Jane, and Anthony Doob. 1997. "Fear, Victimization, and Attitudes to Sentencing, the Courts, and the Police." *Canadian Journal of Criminology* 39: 275–91.

Surette, Ray. 1998. *Media, Crime, and Criminal Justice: Images, Realities, and Policies.* Belmont, Calif.: Wadsworth.

Swanson, Christopher, and Duncan Chaplin. 2003. "Counting High School Graduates When Graduates Count: Measuring Graduation Rates Under the High Stakes of NCLB [No Child Left Behind]." Washington, D.C.: Urban Institute Education Policy Center.

Tate, Katherine. 1991. "Black Political Participation in the 1984 and 1988 Presidential Elections." *American Political Science Review* 85(4): 1159–76.

Taylor, Ralph. 2001. *Breaking Away from Broken Windows: Baltimore Neighborhoods and the Nationwide Fight Against Crime, Grime, Fear, and Decline.* Boulder, Colo.: Westview.

Thompson, James. 1982. "Foreword: Remarks by Governor James R. Thompson on the Attorney General's Task Force on Violent Crime." *Journal of Criminal Law and Criminology* 73(3): 867–74.

Tonry, Michael. 1995. *Malign Neglect.* New York: Oxford University Press.

Tushnet, Mark. 1987. *The NAACP's Legal Strategy Against Segregated Education, 1925–1950.* Chapel Hill: University of North Carolina Press.

Uggen, Christopher. 2010. "Citizenship in an Era of Mass Incarceration: Becoming an Adult Citizen." Paper presented to a special session on "Citizenship in an Era of Mass Incarceration" at the annual meeting of the American Sociological Association. Atlanta (August 14–17).

Uggen, Christopher, and Jeff Manza. 2002. "Democratic Contraction? Political Consequences of Felon Disenfranchisement in the United States." *American Sociological Review* 67(6): 777–803.

Urban Institute. 2000. *A New Look at Homelessness in America.* Washington, D.C.: Urban Institute.

U.S. Census Bureau. Various years. *Current Population Surveys, March 1980–2008* [machine-readable data files]. Washington: U.S. Bureau of the Census [producer and distributor].

———. 2008a. "Availability of Census Records About Individuals." *Factfinder for the Nation,* CFF-2. Washington: U.S. Department of Commerce (June). Available at: http://www.census.gov/prod/2000pubs/cff-2.pdf (accessed December 1, 2011).

———. 2008b. *Statistical Abstract of the United States.* Available at: http://www.census.gov/compendia/statab/2008/2008edition.html (accessed October 1, 2011).

———. 2010. *American Community Survey, 2006–2008* [Computer files]. Washington: U.S. Census Bureau [producer and distributor].

U.S. Department of Health and Human Services (HHS). 2009. "The AFCARS Report: Final Estimate for FY 1998 Through FY 2002." Available at: http://www.acf.hhs.gov/programs/cb/stats research/afcars/tar/report12.htm (accessed August 1, 2010).

U.S. Department of Housing and Urban Development (HUD). 2009. *The Annual Homeless Assessment Report to Congress: 2008.* Washington: U.S. Government Printing Office.

U.S. Department of Justice, Bureau of Justice Statistics. Various years–a. *Survey of Inmates of State Correctional Facilities, 1974–1991* [Computer files]. Ann Arbor, Mich.: Inter-university Consortium for Political and Social Research [producer and distributor], 1990–1993.

———. Various years–b. *Survey of Inmates in Local Jails, 1978–2002* [Computer files]. Ann Arbor, Mich.: Inter-university Consortium for Political and Social Research [producer and distributor], 1997–2006.

———. Various years–c. *Survey of Inmates in State and Federal Correctional Facilities, 1997 and 2004* [Computer files]. Ann Arbor, Mich.: Inter-university Consortium for Political and Social Research [producer and distributor], 2001 and 2007.

———. 2003. *Sourcebook of Criminal Justice Statistics.* Washington: U.S. Government Printing Office.

———. 2004. *Sourcebook of Criminal Justice Statistics.* Washington: U.S. Government Printing Office.

———. 2009. *Sourcebook of Criminal Justice Statistics.* Washington: U.S. Government Printing Office. Available at: http://www.albany.edu/sourcebook/pdf/t600222009.pdf (accessed July 9, 2010).

———. 2010. "About the Bureau of Justice Statistics." Available at: http://bjs.ojp.usdoj.gov/index.cfm?ty=abu (accessed September 1, 2010).

U.S. Department of Justice, Bureau of Prisons. 2004. *Survey of Inmates of Federal Correctional Facilities, 1991* [Computer file]. Washington: U.S. Dept. of Commerce, Bureau of the Census [producer], 1991. Ann Arbor, Mich.: Inter-university Consortium for Political and Social Research [distributor], 2004.

Useem, Bert, and Anne Piehl. 2008. *Prison State: The Challenge of Mass Incarceration.* New York: Cambridge University Press.

Wacquant, Loïc. 2000. "The New 'Peculiar Institution': On the Prison as Surrogate Ghetto." *Theoretical Criminology* 4(3): 377–89.

———. 2001. "Deadly Symbiosis: When Ghetto and Prison Meet and Mesh." *Punishment and Society* 3(1): 95–133.

Wagner, Peter, Aleks Kajstura, Elena Lavarreda, Christian de Ocejo, and Sheila Vennell. 2010. "Fixing Prison-Based Gerrymandering After the 2010 Census: A Fifty-State Guide." Northampton, Mass.: Prison Policy Initative (March).

Wakefield, Sara, and Christopher Wildeman. 2011. "Mass Imprisonment and Racial

Disparities in Childhood Behavioral Problems." *Criminology and Public Policy* 10(3): 793–817.

Waller, Maureen. 2002. *My Baby's Father: Unmarried Parents and Paternal Responsibility.* Ithaca, N.Y.: Cornell University Press.

Wang, Emily A., and Christopher Wildeman. 2011. "Studying Health Disparities by Including Incarcerated and Formerly Incarcerated Individuals." *Journal of the American Medical Association* 305(16): 1708–9.

Warren, John. 2005. "State-Level High School Completion Rates: Concepts, Measures, and Trends." *Education Policy Analysis Archives* 13: 1–38.

Warren, John, and Andrew Halpern-Manners. 2007. "Is the Glass Emptying or Filling Up? Reconciling Divergent Trends in High School Completion and Dropout." *Educational Researcher* 36(6): 335–43.

———. 2009. "Measuring High School Graduation Rates at the State Level: What Difference Does Methodology Make?" *Sociological Methods Research* 38(1): 3–37.

Welch, Finis. 1990. "The Employment of Black Men." *Journal of Labor Economics* 8(1): S26–74.

Welch, Michael, Lisa Weber, and Walter Edwards. 2000. "'All the News That's Fit to Print': A Content Analysis of the Correctional Debate in the *New York Times*." *The Prison Journal* 80(3): 245–64.

West, Heather, and William Sabol. 2009. "Prison Inmates at Midyear 2008: Statistical Tables." National Criminal Justice Archive 225619. Washington: U.S. Department of Justice, Office of Justice Programs.

Western, Bruce. 2002. "The Impact of Incarceration on Wage Mobility and Inequality." *American Sociological Review* 67(4): 526–46.

———. 2006. *Punishment and Inequality in America.* New York: Russell Sage Foundation.

Western, Bruce, and Katherine Beckett. 1999. "How Unregulated Is the U.S. Labor Market? The Penal System as a Labor Market Institution." *American Journal of Sociology* 104(4): 1030–60.

Western, Bruce, Leonard Lopoo, and Sara McLanahan. 2004. "Incarceration and the Bonds Between Parents in Fragile Families." In *Imprisoning America: The Social Effects of Mass Incarceration*, edited by Mary Pattillo, David Weiman, and Bruce Western. New York: Russell Sage Foundation.

Western, Bruce, and Becky Pettit. 2000. "Incarceration and Racial Inequality in Men's Employment." *Industrial and Labor Relations Review* 54(1): 3–16.

———. 2005. "Black-White Wage Inequality, Employment Rates, and Incarceration." *American Journal of Sociology* 111(2): 553–78.

———. 2010. "Incarceration and American Inequality." *Daedalus* 139(3): 8–19.

Whitman, James. 2003. *Harsh Justice: Criminal Punishment and the Widening Divide Between America and Europe.* New York: Oxford University Press.

Wildeman, Christopher. 2009. "Parental Imprisonment, the Prison Boom, and the Concentration of Childhood Disadvantage." *Demography* 46(2): 265–80.

———. 2010. "Paternal Incarceration and Children's Physically Aggressive Behaviors: Evidence from the Fragile Families and Child Well-being Study." *Social Forces* 89(1): 285–309.

Willis, Paul. 1977. *Learning to Labor: How Working-Class Kids Get Working-Class Jobs.* New York: Columbia University Press.

Wilson, William Julius. 1987. *The Truly Disadvantaged: The Inner City, the Underclass, and Public Policy.* Chicago: University of Chicago Press.

INDEX

Boldface numbers refer to figures and tables.

ACS. *See* American Community Survey

Adoption and Foster Care Analysis and Reporting System, 105

African Americans: the civil rights era and, 3; employment rates of young, black men, 63–64; imprisonment *vs.* completing college, likelihood of, 18; invisibility of, 3–9, 22–23; myths of black progress, 102–3; undercounts of by the Census and sample survey research, 30–32; voter turnout by, 70–71, 75–77 (*see also* voter turnout); young, low-skill men, inadequate enumeration of, 46–47. *See also* race/racial inequality

Alexander, Michelle, 14, 39

American Civil Liberties Union (ACLU), 56

American Community Survey (ACS): data collection through statistical sampling, 21; educational distribution of the population, 114; expanded scope of, 28; high school dropouts among young black men,

estimate of, 46; incarceration rates for young, low-skill black men, estimate of, 46; inmates, counting of, 45; institutionalized, estimates of the proportion of the population that are, 113; prison and jail population, estimates of, 31; veterans, estimate of number of, 104

Arditti, Joyce, 89

Arum, Richard, 57

Baker v. Carr, 23

Beattie, Irenee, 57

Beckett, Katherine, 94

Biden, Joseph, 14, 37

Binswanger, Ingrid, 96

blacks. *See* African Americans

Blakely v. Washington, 101

Blank, Rebecca, 51

Booth, Charles, 24

Bowles, Samuel, 55

Braman, Donald, 88, 93

Brooks, Jack, 37

Brown v. Board of Education, 50, 68

Burch, Traci, 72
Bush, George H. W., 39

Carter, Jimmy, 82
Census, U.S.: African Americans, undercounting of, 23–24; geographic location of inmates for enumeration purposes, 92; grants-in-aid and, 25–28; history of, 4, 22–28; institutionalized population, undercount of, 31, 45; political apportionment, counting of inmates for, 28, 44, 92–93; population enumeration by, 20–22, 32–33; undercount, size of and explanations for, 28, 30–32; undercount from 1940 to 2000, estimated net, **30**; young, low-skill black men, poor job of enumerating, 46–47
Central Statistical Board, 26
children: with an incarcerated parent, 83–84; with an incarcerated parent, number of by race, **84**; cumulative risk of parental imprisonment by age seventeen, by education, **88**; in the foster care system, 105; well-being, effect of having an incarcerated parent on, 89–90, 98–99. *See also* families
Civil Rights Act of 1964, 3
Clear, Todd, 93
Clinton, Bill, 14
coercive mobility, 93
Cohn, D'Vera, 104
Comfort, Megan, 88–89
Common Core of Data, 52
communities: impact of mass incarceration on disadvantaged, 85, 90–94;

nonmetropolitan enumeration for men age twenty to thirty-four by education, adjusted and unadjusted estimate of, **92**
Constitution, U.S.: Eighth Amendment, 100; equal protections clause, 26; Fifth Amendment, 100–101; Fourteenth Amendment, 23; Fourth Amendment, 100–101; Sixteenth Amendment, 25; Sixth Amendment, 100–101; three-fifths compromise, institutionalizing slavery through, 20, 22–23
CPS. *See* Current Population Survey
crime and criminality: in communities destabilized by high rates of incarceration, 93–94; growth in the penal population and, 11–12, 39; measuring trends in, 38; media coverage of, 2, 34–36; perceptions of, media coverage and, 38–39; public fascination with and beliefs about, 2; rates of, incarceration rates and, 39; rates of and media coverage, relationship of, 36–38; trends in using four leading indicators, 1973-2008, **40–41**
Crime Bill of 1994, 37
criminal justice system: educational attainment and contact with, link between, 57; expansion of, usefulness of data collection compromised by, 109; health and, 94–98; increased capacity of, recommendations of the Task Force on Violent Crime and, 37; inequality, impact on perceptions of, 11–14; and parallel institutions, history of racial inequality in, 13–14;

punitive turn since the 1970s, explanations of, 11–14, 39; racial inequality and, 54–57; rights of individuals and, 100–101; social exclusion rooted in the invisibility of inmates created by, 101–3; surveillance activities in, 2, 43–44; uniqueness of, 103. *See also* imprisonment/incarceration; penal system

Current Population Survey (CPS): data collection through statistical sampling, 21; educational distribution of the population, 47, 114; educational expansion, racial inequality and, 54–55; employment rates of young, low-skill men, 62–63; high school dropout rates among blacks and whites, 51, 59–61; high school dropouts among young black men, estimate of, 46; house-hold based surveys, reliance on, 16, 52–53, 68, 74–75, 106–7; origin and history of, 4–5, 26; undocumented immigrants living in the U.S., number of, 104; uses and failures of, 33; voter turnout, collection of data on, 70–72, 74–75, 77–78, 81

Darity, William, 53, 68
Declaration of Independence, 20
Democrats, 5, 14
Dinovitzer, Ronit, 88
DuBois, W. E. B., 24
Dukakis, Michael, 39
Durkheim, Émile, 2–3, 108

Edelman, Marian Wright, 83
education: economic mobility and, 54, 68; high school completion, racial gap in, 50–52, 54–55, 58–61; high school dropout rate among young black men, 46–47, **51, 59**; incarceration and, 15–18, 56–57, 68–69; racial inequality in high school dropout rates of men ages twenty to thirty-four, **61**; schools as source of inequality, 55–57; voter turnout and, 76

Ellison, Ralph, 3

employment rates: employment-population ratios for young men without a high school degree, **62**; impact of incarceration and racial inequality on, 52–53, 61–64; percentage of jobless in prison or jail, **64**

families: impact of incarceration on, 84–85, 87–90, 98–99; scarcity of historical data on black, 86. *See also* children

federal data collection/federally administered surveys. *See* social statistics

fiscal strains, prison population growth and, 42–43

Fragile Families and Child Well-being Study, 88, 90

Gamoran, Adam, 51–52
Garland, David, 11, 14
Geller, Amanda, 88–89
Gideon v. Wainwright, 101
Gintis, Herbert, 55
Glaze, Lauren, 116
Goffman, Alice, 31
Goldwater, Barry, 14
grants-in-aid, 25–28

Hagan, John, 88

Harding, David, 85

health: incarceration and, limitations of data regarding, 94–98; status measures for men age twenty-five to forty-four, **97**

Heckman, James, 52

Herbert, Steve, 94

Heyer, Rose, 85

homeless people, 104

Horton, William, 39

immigration detention system, 42

imprisonment/incarceration: alternatives to, 109; collateral damage from (*see* children; communities; families); demographics of, 14–18; education and, 13–18, 58–61, 68–69 (*see also* education); explanations for growth in, 11–14; health and, 94–98; joblessness and, 61–65; magnitude of contemporary U.S., 1; mass, 11–12; mass, myths of black progress and, 101–3; racial and class inequality in, 11, 13–18, 50; risk of, 16–18; as a social fact, 109; ubiquity of in some sociodemographic groups, problem posed by, 108; wage rates and, 64–67. *See also* criminal justice system; penal system

imprisonment/incarceration rates: concentration in specific sociodemographic groups, overlooking of, 50; crime rates and, 39; by education for men age twenty to thirty-four, **15**; growth in U.S., 9–11; "point in time," 16; risk of imprisonment by

ages thirty to thirty-four, **17**; state variability in, **13**; in twenty-one advanced industrialized nations, **12**; in the U.S. compared to other countries, 11; in the U.S., 1925 to 2008, **10**; voter turnout and, 71–75, 78–81 (*see also* voter turnout); of young, low-skill black men, 46–47

inmates: demographics of, 14–18, 58; disenfranchisement of, 72–74, 80–82; educational distribution of, **16**; employment prospects after release, 42; incorporating into national data collections, need for improved, 107; monitoring of, 2; nonmetropolitan enumeration for men age twenty to thirty-four by education, adjusted and unadjusted estimate of, **92**; percentage of jobless, 1980 to 2008, **64**; relocation from urban to rural areas, 91; as socially marginalized individuals/groups, 103–5; voting prior to incarceration, rates of, 72, 74

Jefferson, Thomas, 20

Joest, Karen, 89

Johnson, Lyndon, 70

Justice Statistics, U.S. Bureau of, establishment and mission, 45

Justich, Robert, 104

King, Martin Luther, Jr., 34

Kozol, Jonathan, 56

LaFontaine, Paul, 52

LaFree, Gary, 57

Lambert-Shute, Jennifer, 89

Lareau, Annette, 55
Lopoo, Leonard, 89
Lucas, Samuel, 55
Lynch, James, 85, 93–94

Malthus, Thomas, 24
Manza, Jeff, 79
Mapp v. Ohio, 101
Maruschak, Laura M., 116
Massoglia, Michael, 96
media, the: coverage of crime, crime rates and, 36–38; coverage of crime, political stances and, 39; coverage of crime, popular perceptions of crime and, 38–39; criminals and criminality, coverage of, 2, 34–36; number of stories including the phrase "violent crime" in the *New York Times,* 1970-2009, **36**
methodology: procedures used for estimates, 111–16; sample bias, 5, 7–8, 107–8; surveys, ways to improve, 107. *See also* social statistics
Miranda v. Arizona, 101
Morenoff, Jeffrey, 85

NAACP. *See* National Association for the Advancement of Colored People
National Adult Literacy Study, 28
National Association for the Advancement of Colored People (NAACP), 56, 75
National Corrections Reporting Program (NCRP), 112, 115
National Crime Victimization Survey, 38
National Election Survey, 74–75

National Health and Nutrition Examination Survey (NHANES), 96–98
National Longitudinal Mortality Study, 113
National Longitudinal Study of Adolescent Health, 87, 90
National Longitudinal Surveys, 28
New York Times, coverage of crime by, 36–38
Ng, Betty, 104
NHANES. *See* National Health and Nutrition Examination Survey
Nurse, Ann, 90

Obama, Barack, 1, 8, 18, 70, 72, 76–77, 100, 102–3

parolees, surveillance and social control of, 43–44
Passel, Jeffrey, 104
Patterson, Evelyn, 96
penal system: growth in the U.S., 9–18; growth of, problems posed by, 42–43, 98–99; overcrowding, early releases of prisoners due to, 42–43; philosophy of, shift from rehabilitative to punitive, 39, 42; surveillance activities in, 43–44, 48. *See also* criminal justice system; imprisonment/incarceration
Pew Research Center, 72
Philpot, Tasha, 76–77
politics: of criminal justice policy, 14; media attention to crime and, 39; political apportionment, counting of inmates for, 28, 44, 92–93; voter turnout (*see* voter turnout)

Prison Policy Initiative, 44

proportional representation, 26

Quetelet, Adolphe, 24

race/racial inequality: children with an incarcerated parent, 83–84; employment rates and, 52–53, 61–64; growth in the penal population and, 11, 13–18; health and, 94–95; high school completion, racial gap in, 50–52, 54–55, 58–61; myths of black progress, mass incarceration and, 102–3; risk of imprisonment and, 16–18; wage inequality and, 53, 64–67. *See also* African Americans

Reagan, Ronald, 82

Republicans, 5, 14

revenue sharing, 27–28

Rhodes, Lorna, 43

risk of imprisonment, growth of, 16–18

Rose, Dina, 93

Rusche, Georg, 12–13

Sabol, William, 85, 93–94

Sample Survey of Unemployment, 4, 26. *See also* Current Population Survey

Scarr, Harry, 34

Schnittker, Jason, 96

"school-to-prison" pipeline, 56

Simon, Jonathan, 2

slaves and slavery: the black family, impact on, 85–86; the Constitution and, 20, 22; invisibility of, the three-fifths compromise and, 22–23

Smith, William French, 37

Snow, John, 24

socially marginalized individuals/groups, 103–5, 107–8

social statistics: the American Community Survey (*see* American Community Survey); bias of household-based surveys, incarceration and, 16, 18–19, 31–32, 52; black men, failures in accounting for, 31–32; the Census (*see* Census, U.S.); changing American lifestyles and the collection of, 48–49; collateral damage on children, families, and communities, limitation of data on, 86–87; the Current Population Survey (*see* Current Population Survey); data collection, need for improved, 105–8; history of federal data collection, 22–28, 106; inmate population, discrepancies in federal data sources regarding, 45–46; lifetime risk of imprisonment as indicator of bias in conventional, 16–18; nineteenth-century advances in social survey research, 24; penal system growth and, 5, 21–22, 33, 99; "point in time" incarceration rates as indicator of bias in conventional, 16; sample surveys administered by the federal government, 1947-2003, **29**; socially marginalized groups, improvements in data collection needed to include, 107–8; socially marginalized individuals/groups, underrepresentation of, 103–5; uses of, 21

Statistical Society of London (Royal Statistical Society), 24

supermax prisons, 43

surveillance, 2, 43–44, 48

Task Force on Violent Crime, 37
Taylor, Ralph, 93
Thompson, James, 39
trajectory of cumulative disadvantage, 95

Uggen, Christopher, 79, 96
undocumented immigrants, 104
United States v. Booker, 101
United States v. Fanfan, 101
Urban Institute, 104

veterans, 104–5
voter turnout: by African Americans, history of, 75–77; disenfranchisement categories under state law, **73–74**; estimates for men ages twenty to thirty-four, adjusted and unadjusted, **78**; felon disenfranchisement associated with criminal justice expansion, 72; incorporating incarceration into statistics on, 77–79; mass incarceration, effects of, 77; mass incarceration, voting statistics and, 70–75,

77–82; revised trends for men ages twenty to thirty-four, 1980 to 2008, **80**; trends for men ages twenty to thirty-four, 1980 to 2008, **71**
Voting Rights Act of 1965, 3, 70, 75–76, 92
Voting Rights Act of 1970, 75–76
Voting Rights Act of 1975, 92

Wacquant, Loïc, 13
wage inequality: impact of incarceration and racial inequality on, 53, 64–67; percentage of white men's wages earned by blacks, **67**; white wage advantage of men ages twenty to thirty-four, **66**
Wagner, Peter, 85
Wakefield, Sara, 90
Waller, Maureen, 89
Western, Bruce, 89, 113
Wildeman, Christopher, 87, 90, 115–16
Willis, Paul, 55
Works Progress Administration, 26